The Myste *f My Story*

AUTOBIOGRAPHICAL W FOR PERSONAL AND SPIRITUAL DEVELOPMENT

Paula Farrell Sullivan

PAULIST PRESS
New York/Mahwah

Library of Congress Cataloging-in-Publication Data

Sullivan, Paula Farrell, 1942–
     The mystery of my story : autobiographical writing for personal and spiritual development / by Paula Farrell Sullivan.
          p.   cm.
     Includes bibliographical references.
     ISBN 0-8091-3211-7
     1. Spiritual life.   2. Autobiography—Religious aspects—Christianity.   3. Autobiography—Authorship.   I. Title
BV4501.2.S843   1991
248.2—dc20   90-48312
                                                            CIP

Published by Paulist Press
997 Macarthur Boulevard
Mahwah, New Jersey 07430

Printed and bound in the
United States of America

CONTENTS

Preface: In the Forest of Peace 1

1. Unfinished Stories 5

2. Finding a Way 11

3. Discovering the Persons We Used To Be 20

4. Tapping the Wellsprings 36

5. Choosing Ourselves 57

6. When God Breaks Through 71

7. Transforming and Transcending 83

8. The Mystery of Healing 97

Notes 105

References 109

ACKNOWLEDGMENTS

I first recognize the Author of Grace, the Holy One who led me into my parents' lives. The second greatest influence on this work is the gift of my parents Tom and Margaret Farrell: they imparted a love for words in any language.

While creating this work I have thought of every person who has given meaning to my life. I thank you even if I can't mention all your names. This work began in earnest when I entered the journey inward at the age of thirty-three. My guides, Leona, Rosie, Pascaline, Jim, Kathryn, Patrick and Ivan gave me the courage to keep looking for the clearing where I finally discovered the Mystery.

Writing mentors, Winston Weathers and Marty Dezeeuw, instilled confidence and offered invaluable advice at just the right moments. My colleagues at Tulsa Junior College and the friends who read early drafts provided many constructive comments. The editors at Paulist, especially Georgia Christo, gently pointed the manuscript in the best of directions.

Thanks to Kay and Bob and Diane at St. Francis of the Woods for providing the perfect environment for the final shaping of this work.

Though mentioned last, my husband Richard and our daughters, Amy with her husband Bob Possehl, Linda, and Margaret are my steadfast sources of support and encouragement.

Therefore, most honorable reader, it is not as an author that I would speak to you, not as a story-teller, not as a philosopher, not as a friend only. I seem to speak to you, in some way, as your own self. Who can tell what this may mean? I myself do not know. But if you listen, things will be said that are perhaps not written in this book. And this will be due not to me, but to the One who lives and speaks in both!
Thomas Merton

Dedicated to my brother and sisters—
Tom, Brenda, Margie, Jenny and Julie

IN THE FOREST OF PEACE

Latching the screen door, I turned off the porch lamp that had guided my steps along the gravel path. As I drew back curtains and opened windows, remnants of an October night filled the one-room cabin. A few stars blinked through leafless openings in the dense forest; whippoorwills and cardinals alternated songs heralding a new dawn in the Forest of Peace.

I put Bible and notebook on the small wooden desk and nestled into an oversized rocker to wait for the call to morning prayer. Twenty miles away, my family would sleep another hour. Wednesday, they teased, was "mother's day off," a day I looked forward to more than any other. Too soon these forest days would end, but the pealing gong momentarily abolished the thought.

From cabins veiled among the scrub oaks, a dozen silhouettes moved toward the main house. Birds and squirrels ceased their chatter until the gong's last echo dissolved into daybreak. The day would begin with meditation and morning prayer, then breakfast in silence. It was the grandness of the silence that drew me to these woods.

This was the beginning of my entrance into the spiritual way, into what twelfth-century mystic Catherine of Siena described as "the cell of self-knowledge." In a one-room cabin on a forty-acre tract of Osage land, I first penned scenes from my childhood. In bits and pieces, I wrote down memories that led to the discovery of the Mystery underlying my personal story. The Mystery is simple: the God-force

1

flowing through every aspect of creation and most profoundly in every human being.

Teaching composition had made me aware of, and forced me to develop, numerous ways to stimulate the writing process in novice writers. My days in the woods were spent using the same strategies I used in the classroom. The result was an autobiography that brought me home to my deepest Self. All my adult life I had felt abandoned, rejected, unwanted. For the past twenty years there was little gratitude even for the gift of life. I had stored enough rage to start a war or ruin a marriage. Writing was an invitation to let go of the past. As I wrote, old wounds surfaced and spilled, leaving my body—as if the touch of my fingers on the keyboard or pen to virgin page were salve to memories stored, events needing perspective. So much of what bound me happened at an age when I did not comprehend. Writing helped me look at those memories as an adult, no longer a child peering out of adult eyes. Without my past I would not have written this book. Without the push of anger, I may never have begun to write. All is gift: my life, the anger, the book, the healing.

The healing has come, slowly and steadily. My pain has indeed turned to joy as the Psalmist sings; and while my cry came "out of the depths," God has heard my prayer. Writing helped me begin living the full life God wanted for me from the beginning.

The truth does set us free. What occurred in our early years is part of our truth as adults. Yet, what is our truth in this moment? Do past events have to affect us the rest of our lives? Through writing we can bring those events to the fore and see them with adult perception. The words I wrote in my autobiography are not "who I am as I write this day"— that was me in moments of time many years ago.

In the hundreds of autobiographical pages written before developing the My Story workshop, several themes wander throughout: the need for healing life's early wounds; an insatiable thirst for God; and accepting my life in this world. Four years later, "both" worlds have meshed in a grateful heart. As I reread that material, there is no emotional tug. My life has meaning and perspective. Each moment is just that: a moment that IS.

With pen and notebook, I allowed my perception of truth to flow from the center of my being, from the tissues of memory. Through writing I have found the peace that passes all understanding.

In gratitude for the freedom this process gave me, I created a retreat-workshop, "The Mystery of My Story." The Franciscan Sisters of Perpetual Adoration in Hiawatha, Iowa, provided both stage and audience for a dress rehearsal. The three-day workshop, designed to help individuals write their life stories as a means of personal and spiritual growth, was christened that weekend and has been presented over the last several years in parishes, centers of spiritual renewal and holistic health, and college campuses. The next logical step was this book. I offer it in gratitude to the Holy Mystery in each of us.

UNFINISHED STORIES

The world is very mysterious. It is full of para-doxes and unfinished stories. Many of us try to avoid these paradoxes and finish the stories. Only a few step deliberately into this mystery, into the religious way.[1]

Every person is an unfinished story. By writing down the stories accumulated as we journey through life, we begin to recognize some of the paradoxes, both human and divine, and step into the mystery of "the religious way." Through the telling of our life stories, whether we write them on paper or make audio/video recordings, we create the possi-bility of "dancing madly backwards" into the heart of Real-ity. We dare to explore the unfinished story we continue to create until we draw our last breath. Our stories are not finished, yet writing about the events that have shaped our memories, brings us to self-understanding: the first step in recognizing the Holy Mystery behind the life we have been given.

Through the act of telling our accumulated stories, we honor the events of the past and free ourselves, in the words of Tristine Ranier, "from the limitations of time and place that confine most people."[2] Committing memories to paper helps us to attain insight and discover the person we are at this moment, at the same time acknowledging and honoring the experiences that have brought us to this mo-ment. Writing allows us to grasp fully the significant events of our personal history in an age so inundated with infinite noise it is difficult to experience any moment fully. In the silent activity of writing we come to greater awareness of the Self that is our inner guide and begs for integration with the "I" that is caught up in the dailyness of providing for our most basic needs. Many of us spend too many years mentally untangling threads of experience and lose sight of the religious way.

Writing the story of one's life is a way of actualizing the past and letting go of a natural tendency to dwell on or cling to past experiences. We can mull over events of our lives as we drive down highways. We can (and often do) react to family members and coworkers because they have in some way pushed a button marked "the past." Or, we can choose to rediscover the meaning of our past as we perceived it by making a permanent record of those events. Writing is a means of finding the path that leads back to the only Reality. That path is rooted in self-knowledge.

Autobiography, we might think, should be left to the great ones, heroic men and women whose lives leave an indelible mark—historical figures such as Ben Franklin or Dag Hammarskjöld; a movie star such as Shirley MacLaine; financial giants, Armand Hammer and Lee Iacocca; a literary genius, James Joyce. The most significant autobiographers are those giants who, through the quality of their lives, open sacred doorways: St. Augustine, Catherine of Siena, Carl Jung, Dorothy Day, Thomas Merton. While the words of some great individuals will be found among these pages, the emphasis here is on gathering our stories, the stories of unpublished heroes and heroines: the readers of this book, those who dare to put down the events of their lives as a means of personal and, ultimately, spiritual growth. These are heroic acts because it takes courage to make an honest record of one's life.

Our purpose is to discover the great mystery of becoming, the great mystery of God's presence in our lives. To discover that mystery, we will explore the many contexts of our lives—our personal history in our family of origin, the influences of early years as well as the present situation; our work experiences; our faith experiences. Woven together these contexts continue to create the person we are always in the process of becoming.

Because our purpose is to discover the mystery in our lives, we need not fear creating an account that simply justifies our actions or glorifies the events of our life stories. If we write with the intent to discover the truth in our lives, we need not fear glossing over our less attractive moments or making too much of the grandeur of our lives. If our purpose is to discover the Holy Mystery threading through the events of our lives, we need not fear creating anything false. The intent here is to discover our individual truth that will lead us to the "Grandeur of God."

In *The Man Who Wrestled With God,* John Sanford describes how the Kalahari desert Bushmen were convinced their "stories somehow contained their very soul as a people; and that if any enemy should come into possession of the stories he would have the means to destroy them spiritually."[3] In the West we hunger for such a point of contact with our soul. By owning our stories, having the courage to record and reflect on the happenings, ideas, emotions that make up our lives, we will not lose them to emotional distortion, to the enemy of our public mask: what we, or others, think we should be. Telling the stories of our lives is a way of seeing the source of our being, a way of honoring and thus integrating all the events of our lives. Writing is a means of direct contact with our soul, of contact with the most intimate truth of our human trinity: body, mind, spirit.

Just as the Bible is the story of God's action in the lives of the chosen people, writing our life stories can become a means of seeing God's presence in our own lives. What does that entail? How shall we go about this telling: with pen and notebook, audio recorder, video camera, computer? While technology has provided us with a wide range of tools for recording, writing with pen and paper remains the best means for getting started. Audio and/or video recordings lend themselves more to self-monitoring than writing does. Writing, especially when preceded by memory-jogging strategies, provides more honest results. Something very direct happens as we pick up a pen to write; mind connects to body through fingers grasping both pen and the truth of our experiences. Writing stimulates memory and thought, memories and thoughts stimulate writing.

Other concerns arise when we try to remember the exact details of events in our lives. How accurate is our memory? If siblings or other relatives read our account, would they protest, "It wasn't that way at all!"? We are relying on memory, but we also have to honor where we are as we write our life stories. If we are writing from some distance, we bring something to that event with our later perspective. Herwig Arts describes the difficulties of conveying personal experiences:

> In the ears of the average person, the concept "subjectively-colored experience" sounds like a synonym for experience which is arbitrary, emotional, and hence, untrustworthy. But the average person is the obedient child of an era in which knowledge is considered worthy of the name only so long as it leads to technical control and can be calculated.[4]

Because emotional experiences are easily discounted as only that, and surely inferior to analysis, we may question the truth of our experience. Whatever comes through our fingers, trust that it is truth as each reader of this book has experienced it. Our birth order, genetic history, family environment greatly affect our individual ways of perceiving the details of significant moments. We may indeed begin to question and doubt, especially as we reread our record of early-life experiences. Yet, we can't calculate or control the power of experience as it is re-created from memory. We must write out of our own reality, our perception of the life we have lived, the life we are living. To do this we must believe in our own life, trust our own perceptions. If we look at our life as a process, an unfolding, then from scraps of memory we can piece together the story of our life. When we quilt these scraps together, we see the unique pattern of our life. This requires the opening up of ourselves, being vulnerable, being honest.

For some of us the word "story" may have a slightly negative connotation. It may bring to mind the "stories" we told as children and were punished for our fabrications. The word may conjure up the fairy tales and myths read to us as youngsters, tales that happened in mystical, far-off lands, seemingly unrelated to the reality of our experience. As we experience the events of our life, we do not think of them as story; but when we relate these events to another, that's when "story" happens. We have a powerful need to listen to each other's personal histories as well as a powerful need to tell the stories of our lives. It is in this telling that we come to understand the meaning of our life.

John Sanford retells the stories of several Old Testament figures, without being troubled by the obviously mythological elements in each tale:

> . . . in retelling these tales, I have taken them as
> they stand—neither questioning their historicity
> nor credibility, but focusing upon them purely as
> stories. For from the psychological point of view,
> it makes no more difference whether Jacob existed
> than it does whether or not Shakespeare's Hamlet
> existed . . . it is the story of what happened to
> them that counts, which carries its own message.
> So we will not "fight" the story, but will try to
> listen so fully to it that its deeper meaning and
> implications may be revealed to us.[5]

So it is with our life stories. We need not wrestle over the
facts; the intent is to discover the meaning of these events in
our lives. It matters not whether we have the facts of our
lives down pat, whether Aunt Martha's hair was strawberry
blonde or deep auburn. Whether our imagination takes over
or not, recollecting experiences is what, in the end, leads
us to the Mystery behind our story.

This book is meant to be absorbed slowly. If it takes six
months to get through Chapter Three, so be it. If you, dear
reader, cannot resist picking up a pen and paper, I will have
achieved what I set out to accomplish.

2

FINDING A WAY

When one writes the story of his life and the work he has been engaged in, it is a confession, too, in a way. . . . Going to confession is hard. . . . I can write only of myself, and I pray with St. Augustine, "Lord that I may know myself, in order to know Thee."[1]

Writing one's autobiography may seem an overwhelming task, especially if writing is not natural to the beginning autobiographer. How do we even dare to begin? First, we must keep in mind the goal is self-knowledge, not necessarily a publishable autobiography. Second, in the beginning we take small steps by using techniques for stimulating writing and memory. Before taking up a pen, audio-cassette, or sitting before a blank computer screen, let's establish some distinctions among the terms diary, journal, and autobiography. We will also explore several possibilities for an overall plan or scheme for writing an account of our life story.

The notion of our life as story presents some immediate difficulties hinted at earlier. The *New Oxford English Dictionary* devotes two pages of fine print to the definition of "story." An early meaning of the word "story" is "a narrative, true or presumed to be true, relating to important events and celebrated persons of a more or less remote past." In its earliest definition (from the thirteenth to seventeenth centuries) "story" is "history" as opposed to fiction. It is a "recital of events that have or are alleged to have happened; a series of events that are or might be narrated." Another meaning may evoke some concern about getting to the truth of our life story: "narrative of real, or, more usually, fictitious events, designed for the entertainment of the hearer or reader; a series of traditional or imaginary incidents forming the matter of such a narrative; a tale." While we want to create a true account of our personal histories, sometimes imagination does take over in less significant details.

A narrative is usually created in chronological sequence. This form lends itself to the traditional auto- and/or biographical accounts similar to the seventeenth-century diary of Samuel Pepys. His diary was a literal account of what happened on specific days, most notably on the infamous day of the Fire of London.

> *September 2, 1666*
> *Lords day. Some of our maids sitting up late last night to get things ready against our feast today, Jane called us up, about 3 in the morning, to tell us of a great fire they saw in the City. So I rose, and slipped on my nightgown and went to her window, and thought it to be on the back side of Mark Lane at the furthest; but being unused to such fires as followed, I thought it far enough off, and so went to bed again and to sleep. About 7 rose again to dress myself, and there looked out at the window and saw the fire not so much as it was, and further off. So to my closet to set things to rights after yesterday's cleaning. By and by Jane comes and tells me that she hears that above 300 houses have been burned down tonight by the fire we saw, and that it was now burning down all Fish Street by London Bridge.[2]*

While he is recording an important historical event, Pepys focuses on the ordinary, sequential details of his daily life.

Another form of autobiographical narrative is the journal. Rather than describing only external events, the journal captures what is going on in the stream of consciousness in the mind of the writer: changes of moods, fantasies, opinions, moments of inspiration. A journalist records observations in the midst of an experience; she becomes an audience to her own thoughts and emotions. A journal is best kept on a daily basis, and in that respect is similar to a diary. While the diary records the details of surface events, the journal captures the inner workings of the mind. However, it is not uncommon for diary and journal to overlap. This is evident in Pepys diary:

> *So I made myself ready presently, and walked to the Tower and there got up upon one of the high places, Sir J. Robinson's little son going up with me; and there I did see the houses at that end of the bridge all on fire, and an infinite great fire on this and the other side the end of the bridge— which among other people, did trouble me for poor little Michell and our Sarah on the Bridge. So down, with my heart full of trouble, to the Lieutenant of the Tower . . .*[3]

In the pages that follow, Pepys often expresses concern for the well-being of his friends whose homes were leveled by the fire, with his "heart full of trouble." The journal is unedited, raw material, unexpurgated, as evident in some of Pepys' phrasing: ". . . on this side and the other the end of the bridge—which among other people. . . ."

Journal entries were the foundation of many of Thomas Merton's best-known works. He created *The Sign of Jonas,* an autobiographical account of life in the Trappist monastery of Gethsemani, directly from journal entries dated 1946 to 1952. In an entry dated December 13 [1946], Merton wrote:

> *At work—writing—I am doing a little better. I mean I am less tied up in it, more peaceful and more detached. Taking one thing at a time and going over it slowly and patiently (if I can ever be said to do anything slowly and patiently) and forgetting about the other jobs that have to take their turn. . . . for myself, I have only one desire and that is the desire for solitude—to disappear into God, to be submerged in His peace, to be lost in the secret of His Face.*[4]

In his journals Merton records many of the activities of Trappist life, but his writing always reveals the inner workings of his mind and the growth of his soul.

Autobiography can begin with keeping a journal. If we take up journal-keeping today, later we can return to those notebooks and shape them into our life story. We can edit, clarify, make connections that reveal the themes and patterns of our lifetime.

Journals and diaries are autobiographical because they are "marked by" or "deal with" aspects of one's own experiences. Autobiography is an account of a person's life written by her/himself in a particular form, from a particular perspective. It may relate one's societal accomplishments, reflect only the natural history from one's family of origin, or focus on one's spiritual journey. Whatever perspective the autobiographer takes, her writing is the story of a whole life viewed from the point in time where she begins to reflect on that life.

One autobiographical act with which we are most familiar is the résumé or history of our work experiences. The description of even our earliest attempts to hold a job reveals much about us as persons. Many other types of life events are worthy of noting: school, faith, and love experiences fill in the stories of our lifetime. Some individuals, usually in retirement years, write an account of their life as a means of preserving the history of the family for the next generation. While we can look at our life in terms of surface events only, the intent of this book is also to explore our personal and spiritual development.

The work of Erik Erikson, and more recently Daniel Levinson, provide rich resources for methodically looking at our social and psychological development. John Dunne's theological study of autobiography, *The Search for God in Time and Memory,* provides another kind of framework for examining the spiritual process of life as journey or pilgrimage. The autobiographies of Carl Jung, Dorothy Day and Thomas Merton, among many others, provide examples of life story as pilgrimage and search for Self. This work focuses on the process of autobiography by providing the reader with specific techniques to begin writing. Possibilities for recording the story of our life are many; the reader may select any or all of the approaches offered.

In *Childhood and Society,* Erik Erikson considers the life cycle from the point of view of body, ego (personality), and membership in the community of humankind. He has determined "eight ages" in the human life cycle. The earliest stages, from infancy to the beginning of formal schooling, profoundly affect our psychological and social ease for the rest of our lives. Exploring each of these "ages" as it applies to our personal history is one framework for beginning our autobiography.

During infancy, according to Erikson, we learn to trust

our caretakers and, ultimately, ourselves. We either gain "a sense of self-control without loss of self-esteem" or continue throughout life with an anxious mistrust of others and "a lasting propensity for doubt and shame."[5] As toddlers we initiate plans and mimic the behaviors of the adults in our environment; failure to regulate our impulses at this stage results in an overwhelming feeling of guilt underlying future attempts to work cooperatively in the larger community as adults. In middle childhood, what Erikson labeled "Industry vs. Inferiority," school dominates, and we learn to become productive members of society. If we are unsuccessful in this stage, we develop a sense of inadequacy and inferiority. With puberty and adolescence, "Identity vs. Role Confusion," childhood comes to an end and youth begins. Everything we have learned up to this point comes into question. Adolescent concerns focus on "what they appear to be in the eyes of others as compared with what they feel they are."[6] Writing about this stage in our development becomes a powerful tool for integrating lost parts of ourselves. Rare is the person who isn't reminded in the course of their adult lives of mistakes made during their frequent attempts to separate from family and become members of the adult world.

"Intimacy vs. Isolation" is the stage in which the young adult is ready to fuse his identity with other, to take the risk of

> . . . self-abandon: in the solidarity of close affiliations, in orgasms and sexual unions, in close friendships and in physical combat, in experiences of inspiration by teachers and of intuition from the recesses of the self. The avoidance of such experiences because of a fear of ego loss may

lead to a deep sense of isolation and consequent self-absorption.[7]

Erikson's final ages focus on adulthood. "Generativity vs. Stagnation" emphasizes the need of the older generation for the younger one, the need of the older to guide the younger. Relationships to grandparents are rich opportunities for exploring one's experiences with those who have achieved wisdom that comes as a fruit of aging.

Culminating the seven preceding ages, "Ego Integrity vs. Despair" leads the individual either to the mature acceptance of the life she has been allotted, or to despair that this one life has not been enough and time has run out. It is at this time in the lives of both the known and unknown that the urge to make sense of the whole of life is strongest. At this stage, many autobiographies are recorded in public or private ways.

Erikson's focus is largely on our early development and its effect on our approach to intimacy, creativity or productivity, and finally the ego integration necessary for death to lose its sting.[8] If we use his model for examining the life we have lived, initially it may be difficult to remember what was happening from infancy to entering school. Many techniques for accessing those memories are found in the following chapters. Other sources of remembering early life experiences may come from observations by parents or other significant adults. Erikson's life divisions provide an approach to autobiography on three levels: what was happening to us physically, psychologically, and socially during each of the eight ages.

Daniel Levinson, in *Seasons of a Man's Life,* portrays the life cycle in much broader strokes: preadult, childhood and adolescence (0–22); early adulthood (17–45); middle adulthood (40–65), late adulthood (60–?). Rather than focusing on a specific developmental period as Erikson does, Levinson identifies "eras," or "times of life." Levinson suggests studying "the character of living" during each of these periods. Character includes all aspects: biological, psychological, and social without establishing a focus on any particular aspect to the exclusion of the others.[9] Because the transition from one era to the next "requires a basic change in the fabric of one's life," Levinson allows four or five years for the transition to take place within each era.[10] Examining the preadult era, he might discover connections in his biological development with personality and career development. A young woman in her early twenties made such a connection as she wrote of physical abnormalities that greatly restricted the activities common to her childhood friends. Through the process of writing, she understood how physical limitations helped her develop latent poetic and musical talents.

Regardless of the framework we choose for recording personal history, our story does not end with even the most in-depth look at our biological, psychological, and social development. In the telling of our brief moment "in time," we re-create the experience of our lives and come to understand "God's time" as John Dunne has observed:

Recollection in terms of the story of experience is itself an experience of experience. One reaches the limits of experience with the experience of nonexperience, the awareness of the nothingness from which one comes, the consciousness of one's contingency. One reaches the limits of appropriation when one has brought one's lifetime to mind, one's past through memory and one's future through anticipation. Beyond this, in either direction, past or future, is a time that is really not one's own, though one can in some manner bring this time also to mind. The problem is that time in the larger sense, the centuries, is no one's lifetime. Maybe it would be fitting to call this God's lifetime, the greater past God's past and the greater future God's future. This would mean that in reaching the boundaries of one's lifetime or in going beyond them, one would somehow find God.[11]

In his study of European autobiography, Dunne suggests that the recollection of life experiences allows us to reach "the boundaries of one's lifetime" and "in going beyond them, one would somehow find God."[12] Modern autobiographers Dorothy Day and Thomas Merton examined this discovery of God as they strove to identify the limits of their personal stories and go beyond the borders of their individual lives. The presence of the Other, of the Holy Mystery, becomes the focal point for examining the meaning of their lives. So it is with persons of faith who dare explore their own biological, psychological, social experiences. In that process, they will come to know the presence of Mystery as the connecting thread that gives meaning to and holds their lives in balance.

In the following chapters, we will explore how others have brought their lifetimes to mind and learn practical ways to bring ours to mind, to reach the boundaries of our human story as well as to transcend those boundaries. Finding God is first a matter of entering the cells of memory, a matter of re-creating life events. In this re-creation we will see both the patterns and paradoxes in our life story.

3

DISCOVERING THE PERSONS
WE USED TO BE

> *The memory is a living thing—it too is in transit.*
> *But during its moment, all that is remembered*
> *joins, and lives—the old and the young, the past*
> *and the present, the living and the dead. . . .*[1]

In *One Writer's Beginnings,* Eudora Welty reflects on the richness of her Southern roots which provided her with a "continuous thread of revelation." In capturing a single memory, we are able to unite "the past and the present, the living and the dead."

We can begin with the variety of approaches to autobiography presented in the preceding chapter, yet there are other, less complicated ways to give an account of our life experiences. Whatever plan we choose: the broad areas of life cycle developed by Erikson or Levinson, or tracing the specific categories of school, love, work, or faith events, autobiographical writing leads to self-discovery, to possibilities for personal and spiritual insight and growth. The beginning autobiographical act is keeping a notebook:

> *. . . I think we are well-advised to keep on nod-*
> *ding terms with the people we used to be, whether*
> *we find them attractive company or not. Other-*
> *wise they run up unannounced and surprise us,*
> *come hammering on the mind's door at 4 a.m. of a*
> *bad night and demand to know who deserted*

them, who betrayed them, who is going to make
amends. We forget all too soon the things we
thought we could never forget. We forget the
loves and the betrayals alike, forget what we whis-
pered and what we dreamed, forget who we were.
I have already lost touch with a couple of people I
used to be. . . .[2]

Bringing the past to mind through memory clears away
cobwebs of stored experiences that block our path to maturity. Writing is an effective tool for exhuming those memories and then releasing them on paper. Once this is done,
there is nothing to ruminate about except our new perspective. We are then ready not only to move toward farther
boundaries of life experience, but to transcend those
boundaries, entering God's time.

For readers already keeping notebooks, the process is
one of organizing and editing journal entries into a cohesive
whole. For those who come to writing less easily and have
not kept a journal on a regular basis, the first steps will be a
matter of jogging the memory to discover the myriad, random events in their personal history. The point here is not
setting out to write a complete account of one's life. Rather,
the aim is discovering Mystery beneath seemingly insignifi-
cant events. As scenes emerge from caverns of memory, we
begin to recognize the familiar patterns and themes that
made us who we are as we write. Merton, in his autobiography *The Seven Storey Mountain,* made such a discovery
in writing of his last visit before the death of his brother
John Paul:

John Paul was nowhere in sight.
I turned around. At the end of the long nave,
with its empty choir stalls, high up in the empty

Tribune, John Paul was kneeling all alone, in uni-
form. He seemed to be an immense distance away,
and between the secular church where he was,
and the choir where I was, was a locked door, and
I couldn't call him out to tell him how to come
down the long way 'round through the Guest
House. And he didn't understand my sign.

At that moment there flashed into my mind all
the scores of times in our forgotten childhood
when I had chased John Paul away with stones
from the place where my friends and I were build-
ing a hut. And now, all of a sudden, here it was all
over again: a situation that was externally of the
same pattern: John Paul standing confused and un-
happy, at a distance which he was not able to
bridge.

Sometimes the same image haunts me now
that he is dead. . . .[3]

In the telling of this incident, Merton returned to a
forgotten piece of childhood that impinged on his adult
understanding of his relationship with his younger brother.
As we unpeel layers of memory, and release those memories
from brain to hand to paper, we become creators of another
view of our life experiences.

The time for passive reading has come to an end. The
rest of this book depends on the reader's willingness to join
in the dance. The dance begins with finding a place to write
and selecting materials that suit you. The important thing is
comfort and ease in writing. I have a special room where I
write, far from telephone, television, and household noise.
In perfect weather, I often go to a nearby park and plant
myself beneath a large tree; there I take up my notebook
and pen. For me, ink pens slide across paper more easily

than do pencils or some ballpoints. The notebook can be any variety as long as it's not a small one. I have used sketchbooks, too, because I like using colored markers to draw (awkward as it is) "scenes" before beginning to write, but spiral notebooks are easier to work with when the memory bank is flooded.

The simplest way to begin is to do the exercises as they are presented. These exercises stimulate memory and free the writer from any fears caused by earlier negative writing experiences. Strategies for retrieving information we have stored in our memory are numerous. We can *list, cluster, mind-map, dialogue,* or *ask the journalist's questions.* Let's examine and attempt each of these strategies.

Listing is a quick and effective tool for enhancing memory. Simply jot, as quickly as possible, words or phrases that come to mind about a specific topic or event. Working in a vertical fashion makes the list easier to use at a later time. For practice, on a fresh page in your notebook, make a list of all the relatives who come to mind from early childhood up through age eighteen: great-grandparents, grandparents, parents, siblings, aunts, uncles, cousins, and other relatives who played a significant part in your early life. As you list each name, you may also jot down a phrase to describe an association you make with each name.

Another revealing list is that of teachers who stand out in your mind, positively or negatively, from kindergarten through your last year of formal schooling. Here is one writer's list of teachers:

Mrs. Chain—first grade (sitting in the corner)
Mrs. Whelan—second grade (her wedding)
Mrs. Reece—third grade (discovered the universe)
Mrs. Littleton—sixth grade (adjusting to the South)
Miss Patterson—ninth grade art (everyone is an artist)
Miss Thornell—tenth grade English (read to us)

Mrs. Taylor—high school librarian (confidant)
Behind each of the relatives and teachers on our lists are numerous stories that, woven together, speak of relatedness to others, biologically or by marriage, and relatedness to the local community as student, two vital aspects of our early development.

Objects or places symbolic of particular events in our lives provide more list material. These are places or objects that, when we come in contact with them, make a whole part of the past flood our memory. A dapper gentleman of eighty made the following list during a My Story workshop.

> *toy trains or train stations*
> *blueberry muffins*
> *cigarettes*
> *mountains*
> *gallon-sized wine bottles*
> *sea glass*
> *empty shelves*
> *yarn*
> *rose quartz*
> *mulberries*

Each item on the relative, teacher, and symbol lists becomes a springboard for further autobiographical writing, for writing that enlightens crannies of memory we have yet to explore. What do we do with the lists? One strategy for developing each item is *random/free writing*. This technique has a few guidelines. The trick is to put pen to paper (or fingers to keyboard) without pausing to dwell on the subject. Let the words flow; ignore any interruptions by the little professor who lives in our left brain, waiting to criticize our efforts. Write without stopping for at least ten minutes, or until all thoughts run dry. Simply start with one of the teacher names: "Mrs. Littleton was . . . my sixth grade teacher, a grade full of the trauma of moving from the east coast to the deep south.'' The writer is free to explore Mrs. Littleton's role in that difficult year, or any other ideas triggered by that opening phrase. If you get stuck, sometimes it is helpful to write, ''I am stuck,'' or to repeat the name of the person, place, or thing about which you are writing. One word of caution: throw inhibitions about spelling, grammar, punctuation to the sky. This is no time to cross out words, correct spelling, or dawdle. Just get those thoughts on paper as quickly as possible. Once your memory is jogged, it doesn't wait for the writer to stop and tidy up her writing.

Clustering, another strategy for using these lists, is a technique that is better explained in Gabriele Luser Rico's *Writing the Natural Way.* For the sake of brevity, follow these modified directions.

Take one item from the lists, place the word in the center of a page placed horizontally for greater ease in clustering. Circle the word and then write as many words as come to mind, circling each one and connecting each word to the previous word. Work as quickly as you can, allowing the words to tumble out as effortlessly as possible. If you become stuck, simply circle the original word a few times until another word forms in your mind. After you have clustered for a couple of minutes, on a clean page write the first thing that comes to mind. Using complete or fragmented thoughts (not just isolated words as on the cluster), write until you come to a natural stopping place and the writing feels finished.

After clustering the term *sophomore,* one participant discovered a high-school incident she hadn't thought of since that awkward year:

> *Sophomore year was not the best of years. I was secretly in love with a member of the swim team,*

Sample Cluster

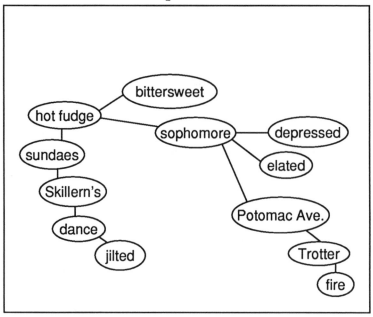

but knew I had no chance. He was too shy to ask. The Sadie Hawkins dance was my only hope. For once the guys didn't have to ask, and the girls were all too eager. Once I made up my mind to ask the swimmer, I decided to trim down at least a couple of dress sizes. Six weeks before the dance I asked him just as we were walking into first hour English. He mumbled an "okay" and I floated. After five weeks of carrots, celery, and dry tuna I'd lost two dress sizes. It never occurred to me to worry about the fact that he never initiated a word of conversation in the six weeks before the dance. I took a month's worth of babysitting money and headed downtown for the Fall dress sale at

*Titche's. On the big day, I raced home from school
to begin making myself look as pretty as I felt
inside. My hair still in curlers at 6:30 p.m., I got
the call. "I can't go to the dance. I have a swim
meet." I yanked the spongey rollers out of my hair,
ran a brush through the curls, grabbed my wallet
and raced down the street toward the shopping
plaza. The red glow of neon fueled my fury. I
entered Skillern's Drug and found an empty stool
at the counter where one of my less popular classmates was running the short order operation this
Friday night. "I'll have a hot fudge sundae," I said,
shoving my fifty cents in his direction. After the
second hot fudge sundae, we were both laughing.
That was the first of many Friday nights I spent
with my new friend. We talked with the counter
between us, but I was happier for being with him.*

One of the surprises of clustering is a seemingly effortless flow of words that reveals our natural style as a writer.
Even the most novice writer will be pleased with the quality of the writing done immediately after clustering. Clustering drops the writer quickly into the depths of memory
where all five senses emerge to recreate specific incidents.
The writer sees the whole incident from two points of view
—through memory, by going back to the actual scene and
through the psychological perspective that comes with all
the years of living between the incident and the present
moment.

Another useful technique is to draw maps of what we
have stored in memory. Developed by Tony Buzan, "mind-
mapping" is similar to clustering, with the addition of
color, shape, and printed words or phrases. The central idea
goes in the middle of the page and all the subconcepts or

related details are positioned somewhat like spokes around a wheel. Before you make a mind map, using a few colored pencils or pens, practice sketching various geometric shapes and symbols. Express the main concepts with key words such as nouns and verbs. Let exclamation points, question marks, and the colors and shapes you choose do the describing rather than filling the pages with adjectives. Symbols may be highly personal. Your maps are not for publication so it matters not whether anyone else understands your symbols. Your first attempt may feel awkward, especially if your drawings were criticized in early school years. There is much liberation in picking up a colored marker and drawing whatever shapes come to mind around the key concepts you have put on your map. Color and shape enhance and bring us into contact with memory.

For practice, create a symbol for each of the following words. Draw something, a shape or an object, that represents for you each of the following words:

knowledge	music
justice	food
time	noise
marriage	war
feminine	peace
masculine	art
God	football

Begin by creating mind maps of distinct stages in your life: early childhood, age ten, adolescence, early twenties, late twenties, up to the age you are now. With color, word, and symbol depict your life at this moment. Who are the people you live with? How do you spend your day? Your leisure? What are your main interests? Through mind-mapping you can also anticipate the future. What would you like your life to be like five years from now?

Elizabeth drew the mind-map on p. 30 of her life at the age of thirty-two.

In creating her map, Elizabeth was able to identify the concerns pulling her mind in different directions. The map also provided her with a variety of topics for more expansive writing at a later time: the importance of relationships, spiritual life, finances, creative expression and outside interests, and self-care. Unlike the writing which is more effectively done immediately after clustering, mind-maps can easily be set aside and used for later writing efforts. The use of color, shape and symbol enhances the memory of what the writer was experiencing or tapping into as he created the map.

Dialogue, an ancient writing technique used by Plato four centuries before the birth of Christ, remains a popular form of writing to this day. Twelfth-century mystic Catherine of Siena wrote her spiritual autobiography in the form of a dialogue between self and soul. William Butler Yeats used the same technique in his poem, "Dialogue of Self and Soul." More recently, Ira Progoff popularized the technique of written dialogue in his Intensive Journal Retreats. For our purposes, setting up a dialogue is a means of allowing our conscious self, the one reading this book, to communicate with our unconscious self where all the experiences of our lifetime have been carefully accumulated.

The lists we made earlier become potent catalysts for implementing the dialogue technique. From the list of relatives, circle three with whom you would like to have a conversation. Then choose one at random. Progoff recommends making a list of details you know about that person before beginning the dialogue. One workshop partici-

Elizabeth's Mind-map of Her Current Situation

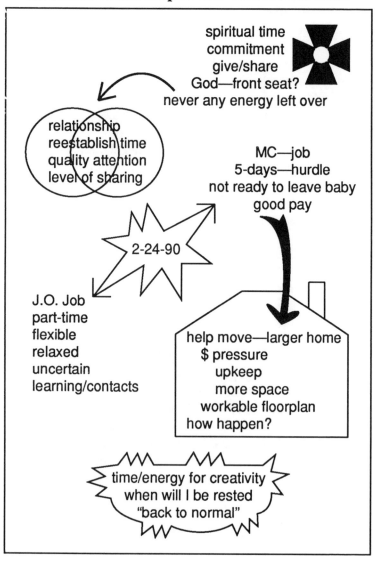

pant jotted the following details under her Aunt Madeline's name:

never married
lived with us occasionally
loved the racetrack and Harley Davidsons
worked as a nurse
never talked about her youth

After noting some details about the person's life, begin the dialogue. Be sure to give each side of the dialogue ample time for responding fully. Here is a sample dialogue.

Madeline: So you think I'm interesting enough to write about? I've been dead so long, I would have thought you had forgotten me.

Writer: You'd be hard to forget, though I must admit I haven't thought of you in years, not till I started writing some of the stories of my life. You certainly play a big part in many of my childhood memories. Remember the time when you and your boyfriend pulled up in our driveway on a Harley?

Madeline: Yes, and I remember the delight in your eyes and the horror on my sister's face. She was furious I wanted to take each of you for a ride. You cried the loudest when your mother said, "Absolutely not!"

Writer: If she only knew I followed you down the block and after you turned the corner, you pulled me up on the seat in front of you. I was squashed between you and your boyfriend and could hardly see anything, but I remember the leathery smell of your jackets and the wind lashing against my cheeks.

Madeline: I always believed my sister thought I was a bad influence on you kids. I loved all of you and would never have done anything to hurt you. I just wanted to have a little fun. My sister was always concerned with being so proper. My life was difficult most of the time, but in my playing I sensed God was very near.

Write the dialogue until the conversation comes to a natural end—usually in ten to thirty minutes, depending on the influence of that person in your life. No matter which person we choose, the result of a written dialogue is always surprising. Through writing we are able to resolve conflicts we may not be aware existed. Always, the writer comes to insight and sometimes to new information as seen in the summary of a dialogue between Kay and her maternal grandmother.

I discovered that I could recall how she wore her hair, the dark tortoise shell glasses she always wore, the generally dark atmosphere in her living room, the elaborately embroidered Mexican shawl draped over her grand piano, the wicker couch and chair on the sun porch and beside her chair the rack filled with astrology magazines. I remembered she baked Shoo-Fly pie and other foods which, as a child, seemed odd and not likely to taste good. But most of all I remember her as never talking. So the dialogue was full of surprises. I asked her about all of these things I remembered and found that she began to tell me who she was,

*from casual details about ordinary life, to revea!-
ing some of the dark forces which eroded her family and influenced her toward introversion and a
kind of sadness in her later years. Her dark house
was a metaphor for the way she closed the drapes
on her own personal attitudes and expectations
and, more and more, lived alone. The dialogue
brought out a cache of recollection within myself
which must have been based on what people told
me about her, pictures I have seen, conversations I
have overheard.*

Dialogue can take place with persons, places, or
things. One young man wrote a lengthy dialogue with an
algebra book and, in the course of that writing, realized his
fear of math was what deterred him from going to medical
school. In his early forties, he had an insatiable desire to
conquer that fear and decided to leave his dead-end job and
return to college to prepare for medical school entrance.
Through dialogue, he examined a "road not taken" and
discovered his earlier dream was still possible.

A final strategy is to use the journalist's questions. Start
with another list: the key events or turning points in our
lives. These may be times when we were caught up short or
were forced to change what had become a pattern in our
living. Progoff refers to these as the "stepping stones"
along our journey. Once you have made a list of these turning points, the journalist's questions will help fill in the
breadth of these experiences. For each turning point, ask
the following questions:

Who were the participants?
What happened?
When did it happen?

Where did it happen?
Why did it happen?
How did it happen?

Jot down as many details as possible for each question. Using a separate sheet for each question allows the writer to return to that question with other details that come to mind at a later time. An early event that stands out in my memory was the day I was lost and found on the beach when I was three years old. The following is an example of how I used the journalist's questions:

Who: My parents—in their thirties; myself, age three; Mandy—an art teacher who had a summer cottage down the street from our home.
What: I got lost during a move out of state.
When: On an autumn day in 1946. It was overcast, cold and windy.
Where: On a beach near my new home.
Why: My parents were preoccupied with moving and didn't notice I had slipped away.
How: I wandered down the street and walked up the beach so far I had no idea where I entered the beach. When I turned back to find my street, I panicked.

As these questions are answered, the writer easily slips into the experience and details full of sensory impressions flow like water. I could recall the smell of decaying crabs and seaweed, the sound of seashells crunching beneath my tennis shoes, the sound of gulls as they dove for their catch in shallow waters. In the writing that followed these questions I discovered the root of my chronic fear of being abandoned as well as the beginning of a twenty-year friendship with the art teacher who found me.

This last example leads into the whole realm of childhood experiences, their imprint on our psyche, their significance as part of the Mystery of our stories. In the next chapter we will explore the power of these early experiences as well as other ways to retrieve and illuminate them for present understanding.

4

TAPPING THE WELLSPRINGS

*Experience is the passive element which is the
starting point for all knowledge. Before I can know
anything, something must happen which arouses
my attention, something which strikes me, something that leaves an impression behind and about
which I then begin to reflect.*[1]

Our life stories evolve from a variety of experiences. Each
experience is bound up in various contexts: our personal
history in our family of origin, our cultural heritage, the
presence or lack of a religious tradition and, finally, our
work experiences. Each of these contexts impinges on how
we view the events and circumstances of our daily lives. We
can easily distort the meaning of an event by ignoring the
context out of which that particular incident arose. To discover the mystery of ourselves, it is necessary to examine
each of these contexts before we can get a full sense of who
we are becoming. The most powerful context for interpret-
ing life experience is personal history, the stories from our
family of origin. In this chapter we will explore some of
those experiences through writing and drawing exercises.

Filed away in the deepest recesses of memory are those
early sensory impressions and experiences of Erikson's first
few stages in the cycle of human development. We have
stored in the cells of our being experiences of trust and
mistrust, of autonomy, shame and doubt, of initiative and
guilt. In the process of writing his autobiography Dr. Carl

Jung discovered connections between works he had written late in his career as a psychiatrist and fleeting images from his early childhood. He describes the sweetness of early sensory impressions of being outdoors and his first remembrance of warm milk in contrast to his illness at the age of two and separation from his mother. Jung was able to connect that separation to his early mistrust of women:

I am lying in a pram, in the shadow of a tree. It is a fine, warm summer day, the sky blue, and golden sunlight darting through green leaves. The hood of the pram has been left up. I have just awakened to the glorious beauty of the day, and have a sense of indescribable well-being. I see the sun glittering through the leaves and blossoms of the bushes. Everything is wholly wonderful, colorful, splendid.[2]

Another memory: I am sitting in our dining room, on the west side of the house, perched in a high chair and spooning up warm milk with bits of broken bread in it. The milk has a pleasant taste and a characteristic smell. This was the first time I became aware of the smell of milk. It was the moment when, so to speak, I became conscious of smelling.[3]

My illness . . . must have been connected with a temporary separation of my parents. My mother spent several months in a hospital in Basel, and presumably her illness had something to do with the difficulty in the marriage. An aunt of mine, who was a spinster and some twenty years older

> *than my mother, took care of me. I was deeply*
> *troubled by my mother's being away. From then*
> *on I always felt mistrustful when the word "love"*
> *was spoken.*[4]

Exploring personal history requires willingness and courage to be open to reexperiencing early events. Two conditions may interfere: fear of beginning such a task or, in the process of reexperiencing, mulling over an event too long. The clustering technique frees us from fear and moves us directly to the experience by the simple act of circling each word that comes to mind for the experience we wish to reexamine. While we do need to reflect on our past, we can easily freeze in the ruminating stage and never move beyond mental attitudes or behaviors learned in childhood. Writing allows us to ruminate on paper and, once the words leave our fingertips, the need to ruminate ceases; we are ready to move to another experience.

In My Story workshops, it is not uncommon for one or more participants to leave after the first break because they fear going back to those experiences of early childhood. A woman in her mid-forties had taken every course for personal growth and development available through her church over a period of several years. Yet, she never finished any course. She came to a workshop and declared at the first break: "I've done all of this. I don't need to do this again." She was afraid to reexperience, "to let reality itself come to the fore; to let it work inwardly. . . ."[5] Out of fear, she walked away from the writing process only to have to face those patterns of behavior at another time, patterns whose roots she could not identify because she refused the opportunity to reexperience them and then gently let go.

> Without reflection, experience is scattered like
> chaff in the wind. Without experience, the mind is
> a mill grinding without any grain.[6]

Writing not only helps us reflect on experience, but opens up possibilities for new experiences. In the act of writing and retelling, we bring the past to mind but then re-create the experience by adding to it the wisdom we have gained since the experience originally took place.

That writing is therapeutic is evident in its increasing use in the field of clinical psychology. It is not uncommon for therapists to ask clients to record their dreams, to keep a journal of their thoughts and feelings between appointments. Exploring experiences of the past is vital to psychological health and spiritual well-being. Writing is an important tool for expressing "what moves [us] inwardly." Self-expression can release that pain of bottling up "an acutely felt experience."[7] Our inner critic may, however, thwart attempts to reexperience the events of our lives. We may distrust those experiences, writing the memories off as too subjective to be accepted as fact because of the way

> . . . the human mind goes to work in an extremely
> selective way to take experiences into itself. A
> human being concentrates attention on matters of
> personal interest and concern. Disturbing or un-
> important phenomena do not then penetrate this
> selective consciousness. To the degree in which
> one's attention is concentrated on an enthralling
> object, the remaining phenomena go unnoticed.
> Some people become so captivated by one aspect
> of reality that they no longer have an "eye" for the

rest of existence. Experience always means "to make a choice."[8]

In the act of writing about "enthralling objects" or those memories we have chosen to remember, we can reconnect those details that seemed not to have penetrated our consciousness. These "blocked" details can arrest our emotional development. One workshop participant claimed she could not remember anything before the age of seven except a doll she loved intensely. After clustering the word "doll," she was astonished to discover, in the ten pages of writing that followed, specific scenes associated with receiving that doll during her mother's life-threatening illness two years earlier. Writing helped heal some of the guilt over ambivalent feelings toward her mother well into adulthood.

As we reflect on the events of our lives it is common for two people who experienced the same event to recall it in quite different ways. Each person selects details to remember and the "remaining phenomena" will "go unnoticed." When the "facts" come together, we realize we ignored certain pieces of information that were available. Perhaps, for self-protection, we chose not to store that information in our "selective consciousness." We neatly packed the unselected material in the unconscious that Joan Didion speaks of, where memories of those "people we used to be . . . come hammering on the mind's door at 4 a.m. of a bad night and demand to know who deserted them, who betrayed them, who is going to make amends."[9] Not only do we make choices regarding what we will remember of an experience, we also act out of our selectivity and make choices that will affect the present and future as well.

One young man's way of coping with disturbing events

in his earliest childhood home was to stay out of doors as much as possible. The "enthralling object" in his experience was all of nature—the backyard, the sky, birds, the mountains in the distance. He had few specific memories of the gloominess that pervaded his childhood experiences, just the sense that it was better to be out of doors than inside. Indoors, his enthralling object was classical music. While siblings disliked or ignored it, he sat quietly near the record player and focused only on the symphonic sounds, blocking out the unpleasantness around him. In writing about his childhood, he began to understand why the mountains and music loomed so large in his memory. In a houseful of brothers and sisters, he remembered little interaction. Loneliness permeated his childhood and early adult memories until he was able to recognize, through writing, the decision he had made: to allow nature and music to become his trusted companions. It was a choice he had made, for whatever reason. Maturing emotionally and spiritually meant accepting the responsibility for those choices. Writing helped him move out of the introspective world of nature and music and become more involved in a variety of adult relationships through his employment and recreational interests.

As adults looking back on early memories, we may fear what we will find. One woman describes an insight gleaned from accepting responsibility for the selective choices she made in early childhood:

> What I remember most about my earliest years, from age three to ten, was my mother's poor health, my father's absence, and the beach. I don't remember my mother ever being well. The door to her bedroom seemed forever shut. If she was visible, she was lying on a couch in the living room.

We were always told to keep our voices down. I remember more the absence of my father than his presence. When he was present, what he did and said I carefully remembered, savoring every harsh act and word. Only in adulthood, when I dared face those years, could I also remember the times when my mother was well and my father treated me with kindness. The ocean remains the dominant force in my memory because I chose to roam beaches rather than interact with my family. Through writing, once the painful memories were released on paper, the waters cleared enough to reexperience those things my parents did to express care, concern, and genuine interest in the kind of person I would become. The hardest part was accepting responsibility for the selections I had made, for the details I chose to select as a youngster.

Understanding the manner in which we psychologically record experience leads to the possibility of accepting as well the parts of experience we ignored.

The stream of consciousness is continually at work. But it is only through choice that one arrives at experience. A person sorts through the phenomena which confront the senses. On what basis is a selection made? Who has taught us to distinguish the wheat from the chaff? Is it really the chaff that is allowed to fall, or even be repressed? And, on the other hand, is it the most important material that penetrates the consciousness?[10]

An area which powerfully affects our lifelong attitudes is sexuality. Is what we remember of early bodily/sexual experiences "the most important material" or should we toss that away as chaff. Dorothy Day brings her late-in-life perspective on what she sensed of her early training regarding morality and sex:

> *Very early we had a sense of right and wrong, good and evil. Morality lay in the realm of property and sex. Violence, murder, all had to do with our relations with one another over property. Sex was a deeper matter, and in some obscure way had a connection with the supernatural law and God Himself. Sex and religion! It was immodest to talk of either. We did not learn shame as children until we learned about sex. Later we were confused in our adolescence, as to why such a consciousness linked up in some obscure way with beauty and love, could be evil.*[11]

Sometimes it is helpful to explore difficult parts of our past with siblings who shared some of our experiences. One workshop participant described what she learned about her past on a weekend visit with her sister:

> *We took a room in a town half the distance between our homes. Without planning it, we began talking about our earliest memories, the first home we remembered then our earliest memory there. As I described the play area of the apartment we lived in during World War II, my sister filled in details she remembered. While I recalled the outdoor play*

area and the scary-looking people who hung around the courtyard, she remembered the stairway on which a rough little boy used to tease and chase her. Many of her memories took place inside the homes we lived in and nearly all of mine took place outdoors, away from the stormy atmosphere of our upbringing. She stayed inside to see what would happen while I stayed outside, not wanting to know. As an adult, I had to find out what was happening inside. Our meeting clarified the uniqueness of our selective memories and brought us much closer than we were in childhood.

In addition to writing about the past, we can share our life stories in a spiritual discernment relationship, in counseling, or with a friend or sibling. After attending a My Story workshop, one participant wanted to find out if her childhood memories fit with those of her younger sister. She arranged a weekend visit to her sister's home and wrote the following on her return:

The first night, we went out to dinner and then to a movie. It took us awhile to reconnect since we hadn't been together in many years. The next morning, we started talking about our elementary school years. I was amazed at what different details she remembered about experiences we shared in common. I remembered all our secret games and code words, but she spoke only of her fears of storms, darkness, and the frightening woods near our home. She was terrified of the forest and I loved it. As the day wore on, our plans to shop dissolved into hours of catching up on our lives.

Late into Saturday night we dared bring up the one
topic no one ever spoke about, the terrible dark-
ness we knew was going on but couldn't talk
about—incest. Talking about it lifted a veil that
hovered over my childhood so darkly I often won-
dered if it really happened or if I had only imag-
ined it. I returned to my husband and children,
relieved that the veil had been lifted. I have to deal
with it, but at least the darkness has a name.

Meinrad Craighead, artist/author of *The Mother's*
Songs and national lecturer/presenter in seminars and
workshops, believes "we are born remembering; we have
psychic connections." She asks workshop participants:
"What layers of our mother's psychic life are woven into us
in prenatal rhythms? Those rhythms are pressed into our
flesh. We see through our mother's eyes before we can
see." Of her own childhood, Craighead writes:

My grandmother was a storyteller. I remember the
telling. Lying in her arms, I heard her voice gather
in the rhythm of the front porch swing, the night
chorus of cicadas, the flashes of the fireflies in the
boxwood hedge. I remember her voice but not
many of the stories she told me. My imagery origi-
nates here, not in the memory of verbal content
but in the pulse beat I learned from her body and
the breath of her dark imagination which I still
feel in the wonder of the natural world.[12]

Drawing is another effective tool for exploring the
past. You may want to have some drawing paper and
markers or pastels at hand to re-create some of the child-

hood images that come to mind as you read the next few pages. In her workshops, Craighead suggests drawing your earliest memories first, without any concern for technique:

1. Draw the home you lived in, the bedroom you oc-cupied, the view from your bed.
2. Then move out into the yard, onto the street where you lived, the neighborhood.
3. Draw the imaginary animals or playmates you in-vented.
4. What did the moonlight look like as it streamed into your room?
5. Draw your favorite childhood tree.

The benefits of using drawing as a means of remembering are numerous as one participant explains:

As I created each drawing Craighead suggested, stories emerged I had not thought of since they happened. From these crude drawings, I noticed aspects of my childhood I had long forgotten. I was quite struck by the drawing of my neighbor-hood. The houses were very sketchy, as if thinly remembered. A narrow path flowed across the page and then downward. I tried to draw a favorite childhood tree, and there were trees in my back-yard, but the trees faded as the ocean emerged at the bottom of my street. I immediately flipped the sketch pad and drew myself as a lone figure on the shore, facing the ocean. It was a moment of revela-tion. The sparseness of people in my childhood memories came from the drawing, and then I re-membered how I spent many childhood days, alone on the beach.

The natural world speaks clearly in our early images. For a few minutes, close your eyes and recall a favorite outdoor place, a place where you felt safe and content, completely at home: a tree house, a park, a meadow behind the barn, a creek bed near your home, a place where you and your siblings or friends experienced the wonder of being children.

What do you smell in this place? What do you see as you look around? Take in each image you remember. What can you hear in this place of contentment? As you reach out with your hand, what textures do you feel? Stiff August grass? The rough bark of a scrub oak? Wet sand? Water flowing through your fingers? Close your eyes and remain in this place for a few moments; soak up every detail with all of your senses. When you are ready to leave this place, open your eyes and draw or write about this special outdoor place of childhood contentment. Begin by naming the place. Write, draw, or audio-record with as much detail as you can, using the wisdom of all five senses to guide you into self-discovery. Once you begin, keep your pen, crayon, or voice moving. If you appear stuck, simply repeat the name of the place until another thought comes to mind. Keeping the pen or crayon moving sends signals to your memory to continue the search for connections with this favorite outdoor spot. Stop only when you naturally sense the end of fully exploring the memory of this place.

As we continue to explore all areas of our lives, the important issue is childlike openness:

> In experiencing, one acts like a child: almost greedily and enthusiastically touching and inquiring about the things being discovered (i.e., selecting or choosing from an unbroken "stream of consciousness").[13]

Workshop participants are invited to get in touch with the five-year-old child they used to be. At five we were greedy for any experience: helping our parents paint a fence, guiding the steering wheel as our parents drove down the highway toward summer vacation, jumping off the high diving board at the dare of an older sibling. We brim over with wonder and creativity. We make up stories that closely model our life experiences and never tire of "let's pretend." Going inside to find our buried child is essential to rediscovering the enthusiasm that will spark new discoveries about the person we continue to become.

Home Stories

Another vibrant source of material for writing is all the homes we have lived in. Writing about our earliest home(s) taps deeply into the first stages of our psychological and spiritual development. In *A Tree Full of Angels,* Macrina Wiederkehr explores the depths evoked by that simple word:

> *Since I do not remember the home of my mother's womb, my first conscious home was the family into which I was born. That home was my first place of formation. I have cherished memories of my parents, brothers and sisters, the country, gardens, pine trees, grape vineyards, homemade bread and wine, poverty, faith, God, Sunday afternoons. It was not a home where I received everything I needed, but it was enough to get me started.*
>
> *While I was living in this home I didn't understand it very well. It often takes a backward, reflective glance to understand the depths of*

things. It is catching up to me a little more each day, this first home of mine, and I am becoming aware of all the little ways I ran away from that home even while living in it. I disappeared a lot as a child. It was a creative way of surviving. I ran away to the forest that surrounded our farm. It became a place of solitude for me, a second home tucked away in the green of the trees.

Not all running away is harmful. Sometimes it is a necessary part of growth. Even now I'm discovering ways that I return to that first home. There is a child in me who needs to be embraced again and again. The reason for my flight as a child came from a wisdom I was too young to understand. Now in my later years I can harvest the wisdom of my childhood. I treasure those precious roots knowing that I have grown wings and I must move on. I must let go. . . . That first home is one that all of us must let go of as we go forth to find new homes. And yet, we always carry it with us. We are all we've ever been as we move forward, in process, to become all we can be. Going home is a sacred journey.[13]

Writing is a means of finding our way back to that sacred home in the center of our being. In order to get there, it is almost always necessary to reflect on our early environment. Doe, a recently widowed workshop participant, discovered how easily pen and paper led her back to an early home memory:

Blue Ribbon Bakery was right across the street from our house. It provided the neighborhood with sumptuous, summoning smells six mornings a week. Its five-cent loaf of bread was elegantly wrapped in slick white paper with a blue ribbon logo drawn to look like a one-pound gift-wrapped package. And its rolls . . . ahh . . . its cinnamon rolls—some dribbled with white icing, some with pink—were the most delicious delicacy. This was my favorite house when I was four. It had a single car garage way in the back with a driveway running the entire length of the lot connecting it to the forbidden street. Everything bounded on that driveway was returned with a snap. Anything with wheels rolled like lightning on its firm surface. And the driveway sizzled our bottoms in the summertime for many sit-down games.

Bobby's parents owned the bakery and lived in the nice white house right beside it. Everything at the bakery was white: the house, the delivery trucks, the uniforms, even Bobby. His parents seemed old and I secretly thought they were his grandparents. They never smiled and they dressed Bobby up every day as if he were going to Sunday School.

Bobby played with us when we allowed and we allowed when he sneaked us piping hot, gooey cinnamon rolls. They were his ticket into our paradise, my brother's and mine. We traded Bobby's rolls for our great company and sometimes grapes from our backyard arbor and the occasional opportunity to pet and feed the goldfish in our big outdoor pond. When a fish died, we blamed Bobby. Daddy said the fish probably ate too many snowball blossoms that fell into the pond, but we still blamed Bobby.

Bobby loved to play with my doll Yvonne. She

had beautiful blue eyes that opened and closed and real eyelashes. Bobby pushed Yvonne up and down the driveway while we napped behind drawn shades during a 110 degree August afternoon. Yvonne's head melted into the driveway. Mother and Daddy looked accusingly at me but I blamed Bobby even though it was I who left her there.

Later I realized I cared just as much for Yvonne with her crooked face as I did with her pretty one; Bobby loved her even more. He cooed his concern for her disfigurement while he lovingly pushed her up and down the driveway and I licked my fingers made sticky by cinnamon rolls.

While Doe set out to write a "first home" memory, her hand guided her mind to many other thoughts: the sights, sounds, tastes and odors from her early outdoor environment; the significance of Bobby as a neighbor; her doll Yvonne's disfigurement and her acceptance of that; impressions of early parental attitudes. On bringing this piece to a close, the writer added: "An almost effortless gushing of words pour forth as clustering pushes those hot buttons of memory which instantly plug us into long-forgotten life experiences."

Allowing the above passage to serve as a catalyst, make a list of all the homes in which you have lived. You may want to begin with your current address and move back in time and memory. Once the list is complete, begin with the first home you remember. Try to describe it in as much detail as possible; better yet, draw what you remember of that home.

Draw each room as you remember this house.

Where did you spend most of your time?

Describe the living room and dining room.
What do you recall of the kitchen?
What was the outside like?
Was it brick or frame? Were there trees in the yard?
Did this house have a basement?
Then make a list of significant events that occurred while you lived in that home: births of siblings, the loss of a friend or relative through death or a move, entering or leaving a particular school, illnesses, visits by out-of-town relatives, holidays, summer vacations.

Having listed these events, you are ready to explore the full significance of each home. Without concern for chronology, choose any event from your list and write as fully as you can about that event. Once you have written about each event on your list, move to the next home and make a list of details about the interior and exterior of that home; then list events that happened while you lived there. While you may write about the same events in another context later on, each slightly different frame of reference yields new insights.

School Stories

Writing about school experiences is an area where selectivity plays a key role. What makes us focus on certain teachers or classmates? Start with your earlier list of teachers and make lists of incidents that happened under their tutelage; include the names of classmates and friends of your school days.

One workshop participant, a high school English teacher in her early forties, chose the name of her senior English teacher to begin this exercise. She was surprised to remember a classmate she had not thought about since high school graduation.

Sister Eleanor had a dry, methodical approach to teaching literature, but when she called on Mary Frances, whether to read or explain the meaning of a poem, time stopped. There was respect in the teacher's voice as she said, "Mary Frances, will you read and then comment on Hopkins' poem?" A withdrawn, plain-looking young woman, Mary Frances read "Pied Beauty" with passion, reverencing every line. The teacher's obvious respect for Mary Frances magnified our awe that someone as young as we could grasp the richness of Hopkins or Yeats. Mary Frances made us love a literature that seemed old and far removed from the cold-war world in which we lived. Eleanor and Mary Frances were mentors for the teacher and student of literature I wanted to become.

Dream Stories

As we explore events of the past, writing or drawing the dreams or nightmares from childhood become valuable aids to unveiling the mystery of who we were then and who we are now as we write down dreams of the past. Dreams are messages from the unconscious to our conscious awareness. Most of us had childhood nightmares or recurring dreams that were so powerful we still remember them. Writing may be the first step toward beginning a continuing record of our dreams from this point on. You may even want to keep a separate notebook just for recording dreams. When I began writing my spiritual autobiography several years ago, I not only recalled recurring dreams from my childhood but began to remember current dreams with much greater ease. Writing down the new dreams provided further access to childhood memories. Many of the associations in current dreams have their roots in early childhood symbols, events, travels. Drawing the dream also enhances the memory and significance of dreams. One workshop participant drew and then wrote of a recurring nightmare that began at age four and ended in her early twenties:

> *I am standing in a field of ripe watermelons. Off to my left stands a stern-faced farmer wearing blue coveralls and holding a pitchfork that is stuck in the earth. All of a sudden, one watermelon rapidly expands and begins to take up my whole world. I wake up screaming as the watermelon takes over all the earth and sky around me.*
>
> *When I drew this dream thirty years later, the drawing showed the farmer and the pitchfork and a field full of watermelons of various sizes. But the one that grew out of control was now a large watermelon that had burst open, exposing its rich pink fruit. Drawing the dream added a new dimension to the telling. I had shared this dream before, but never had I told the dream story with the watermelon broken open. The drawing seems to reflect the richness and creativity in my life today, a life no longer seen as out of control.*

Ancestor Stories

Another possibility for allowing the past to enrich the present lies in the stories we know of our ancestors. Certain stories told about or by grandparents linger in our memories as a rich source of understanding our roots. Sometimes all we can do is remember snippets we have heard from our parents' childhoods. One workshop participant used written dialogues as a means of recalling ancestor stories.

One night after the workshop, I tried dialoguing with a deceased family member with whom I had very little contact while he was alive. My father's father was a quiet, thoughtful person but maintained vital relationships with family members who lived nearby or visited. It just happened I was with him only once when I was six or seven years old. He died when I was eleven or twelve. The dialogue with my paternal grandfather was like talking with an old friend. He spoke so freely and at length in response to my questions and comments about remembered information. He spoke through my pen: "We came up from Texas with one child already born and your father was born soon after we moved onto the land. We brought a few household furnishings—pans, dishes, blankets, a bedstead in the wagon, some books, and seeds and a hoe. We came in the Spring and had warm weather to build the cabin and start a garden. We bought flour and beans and pork in town. Your grandmother worked hard. . . . We knew Indians had been in the area, and some white persons. But we were the first ever to till the land, cut trees and build on that land. There was a freshwater spring on the land and maybe others had found it, but it was always fresh and new to us."

I asked my grandfather why he used to sit under the big tree in the yard after Sunday dinner: "I grew up alone. My parents died when I was very young and I had no close family. And though your grandmother and I had a large family, I never got over the feeling that part of myself needed to be alone to think about the teachings in the Bible and about the great thinkers, Plato and Socrates, and about the experiences after the war and the problems we had in the Territory."

Because we carry our ancestors within our collective past, whatever we can remember is worth recording. The more we understand our roots, the more we understand our behaviors and attitudes.

5

CHOOSING OURSELVES

I shall be telling this with a sigh
somewhere ages and ages hence:
Two roads diverged in a wood, and I—
I took the one less traveled by,
and that has made all the difference.[1]

By the time we have moved into young adulthood, into Erikson's age of "Intimacy vs. Isolation" or Levinson's Early Adulthood (20–40), we have had enough personal and communal experience to take responsibility for the choices we make in life. Many paths, both taken and not taken, move us in directions we are not conscious of accepting. Often we don't recognize the consequences at the time we make those decisions.

Sifting through your own parcel of memories, take up your notebook and make a list of free-will choices you have made from late childhood or early adolescence to the present: whether or not to study when school was your main task in life; whether or not to go to college; to leave home at a tender age or hang around until forced by parents or circumstances to uproot; to marry or not marry; to take or resign from a particular job; to relocate the family; to start a new career; to quit a job to stay home or to go to work and hire someone to take care of the children.

Next to each item on the list, choose at random a color that expresses or represents that decision. Then select one decision. Put the decision in the middle of the page, circle the word or phrase, and cluster as many words as you can associate with that decision. Using the words from your cluster, write about the choice in as much detail as possible. Include why you may have chosen the particular color you assigned to that decision. Continue to choose other items to cluster and write about until you have exhausted your list of decisions.

Ann, a thirty-year-old career woman, reflected on her life choices as well as a recent decision to leave the business world until her children were ready for school. She made the following list of decisions, assigning a color to each one:

chose art class over camp—yellow
not choosing more college-prep classes—black
not pursuing Spanish, not telling anyone why—black
choosing to see Rick against Mom, Dad, and society's "norms"—red
decision to major in journalism over art and architecture—blue
decision to move off campus—green
return to the city where I grew up—ivory
risked pressing my husband on a marriage decision—red
left job at CHP—brown
accepted job at Bell—orange
persevered during job layoffs—orange
chose to open my life to God's will rather than mine—red
worked through trying marriage times—red
decided to have a baby when my husband was returning to school—blue
stay in my home town with poor job prospects—ivory
turned down a corporate position involving travel—red

stay home with my son—red
turned down tempting job offer to continue staying home—orange
decided to have second child—orange
stay within less budget because I am home—orange

After finishing the list and randomly assigning colors to each decision, she determined the following attributes for each color:

red—intense
blue and green—of medium consequence, or I didn't have the only input for that decision
orange—important, but not red
ivory—may be of some consequence, but not an extremely difficult choice
black—poor decisions
brown—low points
yellow—happy, carefree choice

After making your list of life choices and assigning colors, see what associations you can make between the colors and the decisions. Writing about past or present situations becomes a means of thinking clearly, sorting out, making new decisions, or coming to a sense of acceptance about situations that cannot be changed. French mystic Simone Weil understood the value of writing many long letters to her friend and confidant in religious matters, Father Perrin. At the end of one such letter she added:

> *This is a very long letter. Once again I shall have taken up much more of your time than I ought. I beg you to forgive me. My excuse is that by writing this I have reached a conclusion, for the time being at any rate.*[2]

Another way to examine our selection process is to make a list of choices we would like to be able to make. We may find something just underneath the conscious level of thought, ready to steer us in a new and creative direction. Each item on the choice list becomes fertile ground for successive writing experiences.

Roles

Other avenues for exploring life choices are the roles we were assigned, or we assumed, from early childhood to the present moment. Tension often exists between our personal identity and the roles we are handed or take on, beginning with our family of origin, schooling, the jobs we have held, and our situation in life as married or single persons. Through writing about the numerous roles we have lived and are living now, we can define and maintain our personal integrity as we distinguish between those roles that are most nearly who we are at the core of our being and those roles we may be ready to set aside.

Each person is a mystery. Friends, relatives and acquaintances hear our voices, see our bodies, experience our personalities, yet the core in each of us cannot be seen. The roles we play—daughter or son, student, employee, parishioner, friend, parent, spouse—individually do not speak the truth of who we are. Being an employee is not the essence of who I am. *We are persons, not roles.* We take on roles or are assigned roles according to the lifestyle we have chosen, but we are not the roles themselves. In each of us lies a Self absolutely unique. In trying to discover the mystery of who we are, the Self that lies at the center of our being, we can get close by examining the roles we play. The relationship between Self and role is very close, so close we can easily confuse the two. Sometimes others, especially those with whom we live and work, come to see us only in terms of the roles we perform. Evidence lies in the following incident written by a young man in his late twenties.

I easily lock people into the first role I meet them in. A few years ago, I was determined not to spend the rest of my life selling shoes in a shopping mall. I went back to college to prepare for a different future. My sore point was college composition. While I said I wanted an education, I resisted the discipline it took to learn or relearn the basic skills necessary to write well. I blamed much of my misery on a professor I thought was too picky and demanding. She praised my intelligence and life experiences which provided significant material for me to write about, but she also demanded precise use of the English language. One Saturday, as I left the mall where I still sold shoes on weekends, I saw my English professor devouring a waffle cone filled with frozen yogurt as she strolled through the mall. She was obviously enjoying both the yogurt and her companion. Startled to see her outside the classroom, I shouted, "Hey, Dr. McCarthy, you're a real person who shops on weekends and loves frozen yogurt!" She stopped and introduced me to her husband.

The following Monday, things were different. I was no longer stuck in my thinking that it was her pickiness that was keeping me from doing well. I was much more willing to put forth more effort. My teacher no longer seemed so impossible to please. After all, I had seen her wearing jeans and sweatshirt, and I knew her as someone loved by another. She was more than a demanding English teacher. I was ready to accept my role as a student and let her be more than a teacher.

Not only do others confuse us with the roles we perform, but we, too, forget we are not our roles. While on the job, I have to put away my role as mother; my coworkers don't need or want mothering. When I return home in the evening, I must put away the role I perform as employee. The role I play is not me. I am simply the one playing the role. Yet some roles seem closer to being me than others do. I can play those roles without having them disturb who I am at my center. I am comfortable with the role of writer because writing helps me express my deepest self. But some roles make us feel incompetent. Ann wrote about her decision to step out of her career role to enjoy the preschool years with her son:

Deciding to stay home full time with my son rather than returning to work was an "easy" decision, but it forced some hard examination of what that entails. As long as I worked three days a week in a professional job, I still "had it all"—a wonderful husband and baby, a career, money, respect, self-esteem, nice clothes, lunches out, colleagues, an ear to what's going on in the city, business trips, a house, two cars, a baby and a briefcase! I treasured my Tuesdays and Fridays and I had the upper hand in raising my son because I had successfully cut a five-day work schedule to three days and the babysitter no longer knew his routine better than I did. I arranged all the babysitting for work, got up nights and mornings with the baby (except Sundays), grocery shopped, cooked dinners, cleaned house, etc. The company I worked for decided they wanted me five days a week or not at all. I decided to stay home. I continued to do everything but got less and less satisfaction from it as I watched my husband go to Karate classes and relax in front of the television. The role of full-time homemaker was exhausting and who I am was lost under the guise of cook, babysitter, errand girl, mom and wife. At a marriage enrichment workshop, I asked my husband to write down what he expected of me. The top items were things like "playmate," "appreciate my jokes," and "not be high-strung." What a conflict with carrying the household burden by myself! We used to have similar roles to reach common goals. When our roles became so different, I felt like I had lost my soulmate. Our goals were still common, but the individual roles required to achieve these ends were radically different. And I wanted to be more than all the roles I performed as a homemaker.

Roles are indeed related to the tasks we perform: being a parent requires a variety of sub-roles: cook, gardener, chauffeur, tutor, counselor, mediator, carpenter, painter, medic. Each of these "roles" is the result of a work performed in the role of being a parent. Other "roles" result from labels attached to us early in life. If we were less than attentive in elementary school, we may have been labeled a non-student, or a dunce, and then continued to behave that way when, deep inside, we had the natural curiosity of a scholar. Sometimes roles and labels get mixed up. One example is the role of persons serving in church-related positions. Expectations of the role attach to the person, so the person can no longer be herself; she must act like a "religious" person.

By exploring all the roles we have assumed and the labels we have accumulated, we can begin to discern which ones really suit who we are or want to be. Make a list of the labels others have attached to you. Put an asterisk by those that remain with you today. Then make a list of all the roles you have performed from childhood through adulthood. The following lists, by no means exhaustive, are meant to stimulate a list that flows from your life experience.

Roles	*Labels*
daughter, son	dunce
sister, brother	studious one
middle child	dippy blonde
student	nerd
friend	complainer
wife, husband	hypochondriac
mother, father	workaholic
social worker	
parishioner	daddy's brave boy
colleague	mother's little helper
Irish American	teacher's pet
provider	jock
homemaker	princess
cook	frog
writer/poet	air head
	chatterbox
mediator	spendthrift
lover	tightwad
aunt, uncle	saint

Roles (cont'd.)   *Labels (cont'd.)*
niece, nephew
worshipper
employee
consumer

Setting aside your list of labels for awhile, put an asterisk by those *roles* which apply today. Then number each role, assigning the smallest numbers (1–6 or 7) to those roles most comfortable for you, and the larger numbers to those roles you could probably live without and still be you. The lesser numbers speak of who you are inside as well as outwardly, the person you are when you are alone. On my list, being an employee is a role I could live without; my career is not the most important aspect of my identity. I would be hard-pressed, however, to eliminate the roles of writer and worshipper as these roles help express who I am when I am being most true to my Self.

Once you have made your list, as time allows, write about each role; clustering first will help you focus. Explore each role in detail—why it fits, why it doesn't.

Kelly, a woman in her late twenties, ranked her list of roles: "I am lover, writer, mother, cook, Christian, partner, sister, manager, friend, daughter." When asked to select one role to explore as fully as possible, Kelly wrote about being a daughter, a role she felt most distant from in the deepest part of herself:

> *Save for the first seven years of my life, I have never been comfortable being a daughter, nor have I any concept of what my purpose is as a daughter. Because of circumstances and events in my late childhood and continuing throughout*

early womanhood, I would have preferred not being a daughter. I love my mom as a part of my life, but I am not friends with her, nor do I particularly like her as a person. The demands are many and I do not want or have time to meet them. Maybe if there were a book that told me step-by-step, passage through passage, what I'm to be to my mom, then maybe this role of daughter would be a pleasure. Unlike my sister, I have no desire to be just like mom (whether inborn or from environment, many of her traits are there in me); nor, like my brother, do I want to be her partner now that dad is gone. What would I like? In my way of thinking, a daughter should bring unassumed joy, small rays of sunshine, the fringe benefits into a mother's life. The daughter shouldn't be the mother's life. And maybe I think a mother should be a refreshing, soul-lifting trade wind that makes the heat in her daughter's life bearable—not the controller of the temperature.

Through this writing Kelly came to a number of insights. Four months later, having looked back over this entry, she added:

I have changed since I wrote my opinions of being a daughter. I decided to take my relationship with my mother and make of it what I could. The result has been inspiring. We have begun to enjoy getting to know one another. I have learned that she is only human and to not take to heart the criticism she directs at me. I let her share in my achievements and she has a part in my life that was not available to her before. We still have a long road to

travel, but having started on the journey is won-
derful. I still don't know what is expected of a
daughter, but I'm trying to be the person I am and
do the things I think a daughter should. Mom no
longer compares me to my sister and accepts me
as a different individual that loves her in my
own way.

Kelly searched to discover more about her role as daughter, questioning what she would like and seeking a prescription for how to accept her role as daughter. The first writing served as a catalyst for change. According to therapist Carl Rogers, "The curious paradox is that when I accept myself as I am, then I change."[3] What Kelly wrote about being a daughter could not have been said to her mother without great pain and, perhaps, further harm to their relationship. In the privacy of her notebook, she was able to admit: ". . . nor do I particularly like her as a person." Writing about a lack of relationship with her mother led her to the decision to do something about their relationship. Writing led to change.

Relationships

As we examine the roles we were, and may still be, caught up in as we moved toward maturity, it becomes clear that our "roles" usually require relationship with another. Relationships with others are vital to self-understanding. A significant question we may ask is: "Who do those who love me say I am?" Often it is difficult to assess who we are; often it takes another in relationship to help us recognize our true selves. Before exploring relationships, let's look at the types of relationships we experience.

Think of the groups of people you live, work, pray, and

play with as clusters of friends, relatives and acquaintances. These relationships touch your life most often. Have ready four sheets of fresh paper. Draw a large circle on each sheet. Label each circle: "people I live with," "people I work with," "people I recreate with," "people I worship with." Inside each circle write the names that fit with each of these areas of your life. Put an asterisk by each person's name that particularly stands out either because you get along well in relationship with that person or because you would like to improve that relationship. Then examine in a free-writing manner your relationship with each of these persons. Before beginning your writing, jot down a few details you know about this person's life. Now you are ready to write about your relationship.

Carl Rogers explores a number of significant "learnings" he came to during the thousands of hours he spent helping persons in emotional distress.[4] Each of these significant learnings leads to other possibilities for writing. By turning each of his statements into a question, we can list the times when we learned from hard experience the lessons Rogers also learned.

Briefly stated, Rogers' "learnings" are:

1. "In my relationships with persons I have found that it does not help, in the long run, to act as though I were something that I am not."[5] Here roles play a significant part—one test for a role we may consider letting go of is one that makes us feel less than ourselves, less than whole. If I am a teacher and hate to study but pretend I am an authority on a subject, I will feel phony and uncomfortable.

   Questions we might respond to: When, in my daily life, do I feel compelled to act as though I am someone I am not? Around whom do I feel least comfortable in being myself?

2. "I find I am more effective when I can listen with acceptance to myself, and can be myself."[6]
   When do I feel most at home with myself? What am I doing? Whom am I with?

3. "I have found it of enormous value when I can permit myself to understand another person."[7]
   In my past, which persons have I wanted to but not been able to understand? In my present world, who needs my understanding?

4. "I have found it highly rewarding when I can accept another person."[8]
   Who are the people in my life I have come to accept? Whom do I want to be able to accept in my present circle of relatives and acquaintances?

5. "The more I am open to the realities in me and in the other person, the less do I find myself wishing to rush in to 'fix things.' "[9]
   What situations in my life would I like to "fix"? What realities in these situations do I refuse to acknowledge?

In writing about the choices we have made in our lifetime, the roles we have been handed or deliberately stepped into, the relationships we have experienced privately or publicly, we are able to see patterns in our life experiences. In my own experience, my parents' love for language influenced many of my life choices, especially the desire to instill appreciation for the written and spoken word in my children and students. Many early life experiences, however, may push us in directions different from parental values. In all that we discover and write about our past, the point is not the rightness or wrongness of any of it; the point is seeing connections, coming to an understanding of one's life as a whole. Self-knowledge may lead us only to understanding, yet such self-knowledge can become a catalyst for changing both patterns of thinking and behavior. Once we have examined the personal and social contexts out of which our life stories unfold, then we are ready to review the most important aspect of our life, the spiritual journey.

6

WHEN GOD BREAKS THROUGH

*The visible world is part of a more spiritual uni-
verse from which it draws its chief significance;
that union or harmonious relation with that higher
universe is our true end; and that prayer or inner
communion with the spirit thereof . . . is a process
wherein work is really done, and spiritual energy
flows in and produces effects. . . .*[1]

Having examined some of the visible world into which we
were born—our original family and our membership in the
larger community—we can stand back and review those
times in our life when we sensed, if only for a moment,
"harmonious relation with that higher universe" from
which we come. In his poetic autobiography, English poet
William Wordsworth touches that universe:

Our birth is but a sleep and a forgetting
The Soul that rises with us, our life's Star
Hath elsewhere its setting
And cometh from afar:
Not in entire forgetfulness,
And not in utter nakedness,
But trailing clouds of glory do we come . . .[2]

Our spiritual roots permeate all our remembering. William
Wordsworth and William Blake, as well as less celebrated
poets, struggled to express in richly metaphorical language

the experience of that Divine life within. Blake became the Bard, the visionary, who recalled the Divine Word that created us:

> Hear the voice of the Bard!
> Who Present, Past, & Future sees
> Whose ears have heard,
> The Holy Word,
> That walk'd among the ancient trees.[3]

Blake believed the Divine spark is ignited at the moment of our conception and remains the driving force of all creative endeavors throughout life. He found that Divine spark within himself and in the natural world as well.

In his work as a physician, Carl Jung came to believe that the psyche is "by nature religious" and ignoring this dimension, especially in the latter half of life, was sure to invite neurosis.[4] Jung encouraged his patients to return to their religious roots as a means of returning to psychological wholeness. Looking at one's life from a religious perspective may seem an impossible task, especially if we were not raised in a religious tradition. Even if our early years were steeped in religious traditions, we may not have had what we would call "religious" experiences.

The manifestations of God's intervention and interaction in the daily lives of the Hebrews are plentiful. The writers of sacred scripture knew nothing of the cosmos as we know it today, yet they wrote with a firm belief that Yahweh played an active role in both ordinary and extraordinary events in the lives of the Israelites. They recorded "signs" and "wonders" such as plagues, the parting of the Red Sea, and the power of the Ark of the Covenant to make armies lie down in defeat. Because of their belief in God's active presence, they could see the mind and will of God in such ordinary events as the birth of a child or the passing of a storm cloud. Life in the twentieth century, so filled with the distractions of new technologies, makes it difficult to see the hand of God. Once we have reflected on surface events as well as incidents that evoke more emotional responses, it is important to re-vision those times when we experienced a sense of God's presence beneath the surface of our life. Examining pieces from the lives of published and unpublished autobiographers may stimulate memories of our own experiences of that Divine presence.

As young children, the stillness of a starry night, the fragrance of wildflowers on an August evening, the first sight of the ocean may have evoked a sense of being enfolded by an all-powerful Other. God comes, enters our lives in the concreteness of daily activities, both personal and communal. Throughout childhood, we recapture glimpses of the other world. Children greedily inhale the natural world and invest it with near-magical powers; they can still taste the eternal before developing a vocabulary to express what they innately know but cannot define. Jung described his childhood sense of the sacred:

> I also recall from this period (seven to nine) that I was fond of playing with fire. In our garden there was an old wall built of large blocks of stone, the interstices of which made interesting caves. I used to tend a little fire in one of these caves, with other children helping me; a fire that had to burn forever and therefore had to be constantly maintained by our united efforts, which consisted in gathering the necessary wood. No one but myself was allowed to tend this fire. Others could light other

fires in other caves, but these fires were profane
and did not concern me. My fire alone was living
and had an unmistakable aura of sanctity.[5]

In writing of her early experiences of the natural
world, a teacher pinpointed her earliest discovery of that
larger presence:

I escaped to the beach one October afternoon. My
older sisters were in school and the younger ones
were napping. The beach was deserted. I played
with the waves, daring them to cover my red
canvas shoes. Suddenly I became fascinated with a
wave that caught my eye way out beyond the buoy,
our safeguard against swimming too far from
shore. I gave the wave my full attention while it
spiraled back and forth, finally reaching the tip of
my red canvas shoes. Backing up enough to escape
even the strongest wave, I stared into the ocean. A
strange sense of comfort surrounded me as I con-
centrated on one wave at a time. I struggled to
understand how the waves got to shore and imagined a figure behind the horizon whose one task
was to nudge the waves to shore by gently, yet
forcefully, pushing a strong wind through deep
red lips. I mused this gentle person, both man and
woman, wore a long white tunic and had long
white hair and an old yet radiant face. When this
figure tired, the waves would surely stop coming
to shore. As the sun drifted behind the horizon, I
rose from the wet sand. An unexplainable joy
washed over my body and I was fully awake to the
vastness of the ocean. Suddenly, I felt very loved.

*My new friend behind the horizon would continue
to comfort each time I went to the beach.*

As adults, we may be inclined to think of spiritual experiences as those times we felt prayerful, perhaps at some
ritual or ceremony in a church. More often, however, our
strongest religious impulses happen in more humble situations. A young mother wrote of her earliest religious
memory:

*Summer, in my backyard, when I was four con-
tained a fullness and richness I will never know
again. The pure awe of enjoying life and having
time to savour the smallest detail, yet innocent
enough to believe that all is good and life would
always be like this. I believed I was a princess, for
how else could I be given a yard with wonders to
explore. Why else would birds come and sit on my
powerline? Only castles had such wondrously
smooth porches and rough sidewalks, only kings
flew a plane over their house to wave at their
daughter every day. Weren't princesses protected
all the time by the loving all-seeing, all-knowing
eyes of their mother, and wasn't it only in fairy
tales that a girl of four could own the sun, sky,
clouds and wind?*

The sense of mystical, all-powerful figures, whether
imagined at the water's edge or in the guise of an all-seeing,
all-knowing mother, gradually gives way to a more anthro-
pomorphic notion of God as we move more deeply into the
things of this world. Young children, as Wordsworth re-
minds us, are partial to both worlds. As adolescence begins,

according to Benedict Groeschel, the maturing youngster "increasingly uses the mind rather than the emotions to make sense out of life."[6] In a recent My Story workshop, two women in their mid-thirties described their spiritual transitions from childhood to adulthood:

Jennifer's Story

I always knew God existed. I don't remember a specific time of awakening. It's like I always knew and never questioned the possibility of God not existing. I saw the sky and birds and flowers and knew God was there. In church I got the traditional "God is everywhere and he is watching you all the time" stuff. I remember thinking, "Impossible!" When I was baptized into the church, I did feel a deep sense of emotion—it was almost more an act of courage to step forward and say I believe in God. It did come from deep inside. I couldn't stay seated. In my early teen years I grew away from the church. I never stopped believing in God, but I saw no need to go to church with hypocrites. I still prayed, usually when I was scared for myself or for others. Somehow my concept evolved from the big man in the sky to an energy or force present in everything and everyone. I do not recall any certain event that precipitated this change. When my grandparents died, I felt tremendous grief, but at the same time they lived on inside me, their spirits were still alive.

My current belief in God is still evolving. I believe in a force or energy in the universe. I know this force to be present when I get still and look at my world. There has to be something that keeps order. The seasons change; day becomes night and new life is created on a regular basis. This is evidence of God. I see God in children and ragged old men. My current beliefs come from a variety of sources. Oriental philosophy, Christianity and my own intuition lead me to believe as I do. I have seen miracles with my own eyes. For me, God is a felt attitude that lies deep inside a person. God is love, God is all beauty. God is Divine Order of the Universe. When I get very still, I feel a Presence. This is God.

Michelle's Story

As a very young child, I was fascinated by Joan of Arc. It was a mystery to me that she could be who she was. She had to be like a man. She heard the voices; they spoke to her, guided her. And she was condemned. So God was these voices that spoke, that said things, that knew, that helped. But it was also something secret and private.

Throughout childhood I asked questions when I felt in darkness; I asked for those voices. By the time I entered high school, I felt I was being sent mixed messages. My experience was judged as wrong. To experience God meant giving up control. There was healing in that, but it was also mysterious and secretive. In high school, when I split away from my family's religion, my relationship with God became more secret. It was allowing the voices to speak, it was mystery and adventure and miracles; it was personal and it was not.

Today, my faith life is experiential. It is more alive in the context of two or three gathered together that my faith is personalized.

As adults, caught up in obligations and responsibilities, it may be more in times of sickness or physical confinement that we turn toward the Divine. Existentialist Kierkegaard saw illness and physical confinement as afflictions that lead to the possibility of conversion, to transformations in consciousness.

Affliction is able to drown out every earthly voice, that is precisely what it has to do, but the voice of eternity within a person it cannot drown. . . . It is the voice of eternity within which demands to be heard, and to make a hearing for itself it makes use of the loud voice of affliction. Then when by the aid of affliction all irrelevant voices are brought to silence, it can be heard, this voice within.[7]

The apostle Paul had to be struck blind before he could see the horror of his persecution toward the new Christian community. A recent workshop participant described how her toddler lifted the veil from her faith at a time of great psychological suffering and wavering in her beliefs.

Just before the birth of our third child, my mother's long illness became critical. I received a call saying she had six to twelve hours to live. Since I was literally ready to deliver, I could do nothing. Our three-year-old tugged at my skirt as I faced the kitchen window, trying to hide my sadness. She wanted to know why I was crying. I told her I would miss Nana. Her response was a puz-

zled look, "You said heaven was wonderful." She left the kitchen and shut herself up in her room while I finished washing the breakfast dishes. Minutes later she came out and announced, "I just talked to God and he said we could have Nana back. He just wanted to hold her for a few minutes. I told him you were very sad." I hugged my daughter, never believing her prayer would be answered. Our new daughter was born the next morning. As I was being wheeled into my room, the phone was ringing. My father wanted me to know Mother had come out of the coma the afternoon before. It was not so much that my mother lived through that crisis. What mattered was my change in attitude. I was given the grace to see through the eyes of a believing child. Years later, when my mother actually died, my faith was restored enough to celebrate her death rather than pine over it.

Recalling individuals who touched our lives at the moments when we were most in need of grace is one way of exploring faith events. The writers of Hebrew and New Testament scriptures relate story after story of such faith events. These writers used a variety of metaphors to describe the presence of God: the burning bush, the cloud hovering above and before the wanderers in the wilderness, the messiah, the lamb of God, the good shepherd. Today these symbols seem to have lost their power to evoke that sense of God. Part of our spiritual anxiety, according to mythologist Joseph Campbell, results from a lack of connection with those ancient symbols. Important to our spiritual development are the symbolic connections we make, the metaphors that become part of our personal history.

Biblical metaphors such as lord, king, lamb of God, priest, may be difficult for modern people, especially women, to identify with. What metaphors represent our experience of God as creator, lord, king, dwelling in the world as well as within each of us?

In her autobiography, Dorothy Day described God as a "tremendous force, a frightening impersonal God, a Voice, a Hand stretched out to seize me, his child, and not in love. I did not think of Jesus as God."[8]

After clustering the phrase, "Metaphors for God," a man in his mid-thirties explored some of his symbolic religious experience:

> *The most powerful metaphor for me is* Creator. *I have trouble with* Father *since my earthly father was not a model of God for me as a young child.* Creator *evokes that powerful but kindly figure who breathed the winds I felt all around me on long walks in the woods near my childhood home.* King *I have difficulty with because of the poverty —both physical and spiritual in my upbringing.* Lord *is more appealing as I have love for the medieval, for acquiescing to one I want to surrender my will to—but not "lord over" in the sense of wielding authority. Kingly may fit more in the sense of regal, divine, like the seventh-century spirit of kingly generosity. The generous king was loyally followed and his generosity in material goods reflected his generous spirit.*
>
> *Yet, the word* Creator *is all-encompassing. Creator evokes a miraculous and continuous energy poured into me and the universe, second by second. God the creator is a bolt of lightning that*

fills me with enough energy to radiate outward, fill all I encounter with zapping light, the burn that doesn't kill but "scares" into life, a mysterious bolt that comes without storm and so unexpectedly. Lamb of God and priest evoke the least response. I have never lived on a farm and lambs are only furry figures in story books. I don't see much to hang my hat on. Priest feels exclusive, yet the term priestly people includes all of us. The underlying reality of God with us lives in my personal experiences even though I am often times unaware. Redeemer has power because I have such a desire and need for redemption.

If I could create a symbol to express the helping, nourishing, feeding role of God-with-us, it would be a massive, gentle earth mother who enfolds her offspring with warmth and love, protecting them from outside harm; a nursing mother who never pushes her child away, a goddess of great wisdom and beauty, a simple kind of beauty, eyes that smile Love into anyone receiving their gaze. Life-giver is feminine; it's flesh and blood delivery and deliverance from the darkness of our lives, it's Spirit breathed into me at the moment of my coming into the world.

As we reflect on our own faith experiences, we begin to sense the mystery behind all events of our life; we sense more fully the spiritual threads that bind our lifetime in God's time. While we can record experiences within the institutional church to which we may belong, the focal point is individual religious experience. Alister Hardy defines religious experience as the "sense of a larger presence . . . some power outside [ourselves] illuminating [our] life, of having a sense of oneness with creation that results in a new sense of love for others."[9]

Writing Suggestions

Reserve a section in your notebook for describing your spiritual moments. When have you experienced God's manifestation to you through some person or event? List the times in your life when help did arrive, when your prayers were answered in the form of another person reaching out to you.

In a free-write of ten to fifteen minutes, speak to those traditional metaphors for God mentioned earlier; choose those metaphors that most nearly reflect your experience. Then try creating some new metaphors that speak to your present relationship with God.

7

TRANSFORMING AND TRANSCENDING

> *By standing imaginatively on the edge of time and the natural order, the soul's historian strives to repossess his or her time-bound self in the act of moving toward timelessness. Thus the purpose of writing personal history becomes twofold: to share with others the discovery of all that is within one's humanity and then, in a sense, to extinguish that self in what Thomas Merton calls . . . "the clean desire for death."*[1]

The act of writing our personal history up to this point has centered on self-awareness; yet the aim of this kind of writing lies in self-forgetfulness, in transcending our personal stories. Retelling our life story is a means of letting go of self and entering the spiritual way. It is not enough simply to write about events that served as turning points, events that changed attitudes and deepened our level of faith. By sharing our stories and listening to another's, we transcend the boundaries of self and move toward understanding the timelessness of God's life in all human beings. We objectify our experiences and move beyond them to "I—Thou" relationships within the larger community and with the Other who calls us into the deepest of relationships. We move from what Merton calls "the surface of the sea," to the "inner cave" of our being. If we persevere in the religious way, we may come to that "positive life swimming in the rich darkness which is" where "God is adored."[2]

Spiritual writers since the earliest times have indicated

the path leading to the no-place where the Holy Mystery is found. Meditation is one means of entering that place. Writing, too, can help access those "deepest caverns" of experience where God resides. The following exercises and samplings from published and unpublished autobiographies serve as support and inspiration for entering those deep caverns of experience.

Using Sacred Scripture

Another way to explore one's lifetime is through God's time. A record of God's time is found in the scriptures and can be fully brought to mind by reflecting on passages, then responding from personal experience. One means of doing this is to create a "dialectic" with a passage from scripture using the following format. The example is borrowed from Rachel's scripture journal.

Scripture Journal

Passage quoted	Paraphrase (put in our own words)
Mt. 24:42. So, stay awake because you do not know the day when your master is coming. You may be quite sure of this that if the householder had known at what time of the night the burglar would come, he would have stayed awake and not have	*Jesus is asking his disciples to be ready when the messiah is to establish his kingdom on earth. If we knew when a thief was going to strike, we would be alert for the moment and would prevent his entrance into our home.*

Scripture Journal (Continued)

Passage quoted	Paraphrase (put in our own words)

allowed anyone to break
through the walls of his
house.

Response

Even though Matthew recorded these words of Jesus thousands of years ago, they have meaning for me, too. While God's presence in me is a gift, I want to be prepared to receive his grace at any time. I want to be awake to the possibilities of his presence in my life, whether that is through some other person entering my life and my being able to recognize the Christ in her, or whether it is to be ready for my own death. While out walking one summer morning, I met a person of the streets who asked only a light for a cigarette he had found on the jogging trail. His clear blue eyes pierced my soul momentarily. When I had produced a match, I was embarrassed by his gratitude; it was I who had received in that exchange. It was a messiah moment.

Writing with the Psalms

O Lord, you have probed me and you know me;
you know when I sit and when I stand;
you understand my thoughts from afar.

My journeys and my rest you scrutinize,
with all my ways you are familiar [Psalm 139:1–3].

Take one verse of any psalm that strikes a chord of experience. In a quiet place, read the verse over and over until you sense the internal rhythm of the psalmist. Copy the verse into your notebook exactly as it is written. In a ten-to-fifteen-minute free writing, respond as fully as you can to that verse. What memories does the verse evoke? When have you "tasted" the words of the psalmist before? How can you relate this verse to your current situation?

Identifying My Story with Gospel-Story

Now there is in Jerusalem at the Sheep [Gate] a pool called in Hebrew Bethesda, with five porticoes. In these lay a large number of ill, blind, lame and crippled. One man was there who had been ill for thirty-eight years. When Jesus saw him lying there and knew that he had been ill for a long time, he said to him, "Do you want to be well?" The sick man answered him, "Sir, I have no one to put me into the pool when the water is stirred up; while I am on my way, someone else gets down there before me." Jesus said to him, "Rise, take up your mat, and walk." Immediately the man became well, took up his mat, and walked [John 5:2–9].

Read this passage from the Gospel of John several times until you become familiar with all the details. Try to imagine yourself as a person who wants to enter the pool. Write about that experience as if this scene were happening in your life today. Where would the pool be located? Who would be your companions? From what are you suffering?

Do you want to be well? Write as fully as you can, using as many of the senses as possible: what do you see, hear, smell, touch, taste in your scene?

Catherine's Story

The following portion of John's gospel served as a catalyst for assimilating as well as letting go of a difficult few years for Catherine, a thirty-seven-year-old spouse, mother and social worker. Catherine wrote this piece on the last afternoon of a three-day My Story retreat.

"Whoever loves me will keep my word, and my Father will love him, and we will come to him and make our dwelling with him. Whoever does not love me does not keep my words; yet the word you hear is not mine but that of the Father who sent me.

I have told you this while I am with you. The Advocate, the Holy Spirit that the Father will send in my name—he will teach you everything and remind you of all that [I] told you. Peace I leave with you; my peace I give to you. Not as the world gives do I give it to you. Do not let your hearts be troubled or afraid. You heard me tell you, 'I am going away and I will come back to you.' If you loved me, you would rejoice that I am going to the Father; for the Father is greater than I. And now I have told you this before it happens, so that when it happens you may believe. I will no longer speak much with you, for the ruler of the world is coming. He has no power over me, but the world must know that I love the Father and that I do just as the Father has commanded me. Get up, let us go.

Catherine wrote:

> *This passage resonates so deeply with my experi-*
> *ence of God as Father, Son and Spirit. Looking*
> *back nearly forty years, I see how God came to live*
> *with me at quite an early age; I wanted to follow*
> *God even during, and in spite of, times when I*
> *acted out of my own darkness and the darkness*
> *that hung over my upbringing. The mountains in*
> *my earliest years and a city park in middle child-*
> *hood, were the places God touched me most*
> *memorably. In these places, I often experienced a*
> *sort of "passing over" that words could not ex-*
> *plain, but I knew was more than my imagination. I*
> *had no name for what happened; it just filled me*
> *with a sense of well-being. Those were the mo-*
> *ments when I felt loved by someone more real*
> *than anything in my daily life. So much of my life*
> *seemed a lie. My family seemed normal to out-*
> *siders, but they didn't know about the alcohol and*
> *the fights that followed, and the long silences that*
> *followed the fights. But lying on the floor of a*
> *wooden merry-go-round, I gazed into clear blue*
> *skies, patterned with leaves of swaying trees and*
> *experienced truth in another way. I came away*
> *from these moments feeling creative; I wanted to*
> *draw, sing, write a poem.*
>
> *As a teenager, those times of "passing over"*
> *happened less often. I wasn't interested in any-*
> *thing but being on my own. When I finally made*
> *it—husband, kids, job—I had no time for this God*
> *who used to touch me. Then on my thirtieth*
> *birthday, the "passing over" occurred again as I*
> *stood in line at the grocery store. It was time to pay*

attention and commit to a more spiritual way of living. Yet, I had no sense of Jesus any deeper than the historical person I heard about in Sunday services. Mentally I understood, "In the beginning was the Word," but involvement with family, work, and church activities kept me too busy to "taste and see" who this Jesus is. I had felt a stranger in my own church so long that I turned to Eastern teachings. The opportunity came to make a Zen retreat. During those days, I tasted Jesus so fully that I hardly remember not knowing him directly. My knowledge of Jesus as savior, brother, friend was so direct I was totally certain of the resurrection, and all the anxiety about death I had carried for years gradually dissolved. If anything, I looked forward to the endtime and meeting him face to face. In the months following that direct experience of Christ, he spoke often through scriptures and spiritual friendships. Never had I known such peace. It was a peace uncommon in my busy world.

Jesus in this passage was speaking to his disciples, yet I have experienced what he said about sending "the Advocate, the Holy Spirit," to teach me everything and to remind me of what Jesus said so directly in my spirit. I needed a reminder because I sometimes forget how close Jesus is to me. I forget when I am acting compulsively, when I try to control others, when I run from self-knowledge that begs for admission.

The peace he bequeathed was followed by the command: "Do not be troubled or afraid." That was a warning I most needed. After many months, darkness set in. Peace was no longer a "felt" experience. I had to recite those lines often—my peace I leave you, my peace is gift for you, so don't be frightened. Before the peace faded, I would not have understood why the gift of peace was followed by, "Don't be troubled or afraid."

While Jesus was speaking literally of going to the Father, I see why, for my own spiritual growth, Jesus had to "retreat" that I might let go and surrender my own will. He had touched me and was leading me back, although through a dark passage, to the Father, both my biological father and the Creator of all.

For two years I tasted his words, "I shall not talk to you any longer." Where had he gone? I had only the memory of his presence. At first I fervently sought his return. I didn't understand what was meant by, "If you loved me, you would have been glad to know that I am going to the Father, for the Father is greater than I." I had come to desire and love Jesus because of the gift he had given, not for himself. When he seemed to go away, I was called to truthfulness. In my near despair and loneliness, I turned to a greater involvement with friends and family.

I could no longer hang on to the memory of his divine touch. He had gone. I was hurt and angry because I could no longer hear the Spirit. I depended on others for my identity, for my sense of direction. I did not trust or appreciate my deepest self because I did not realize that is the nowhere place that God dwells in me. I kept looking outside, in techniques of prayer, mantras, daily visits to my church, while forgetting God is indwelling. *Friends, family and job did not satisfy, so I withdrew inside only to discover God had never left me. When I fully surrendered, Jesus returned, not suddenly, but as quietly and "courteously" as he had left, almost unnoticeably. The prince of this world had nearly won. I didn't realize how far off the path and into my own image of God I had gotten.*

In that surrender, the power of the prince of the world over my spirit was released. My desire to be with God meant I would live thoroughly in this world until I was called by the Father. In returning to life in this world, I began to heal, gradually, and so did all the wounds inflicted by others, and those self-inflicted. I had to acknowledge the pride that compelled me to move away from others. Stripped, I was ready to acknowledge my poverty. For months afterwards my brain seemed dead, I wondered if I would ever think again. In reaching out to others, with no expectation of return, I began to love for the first time. I stopped worrying about what I would "do." I simply woke up each morning and embraced the life I was seeing with new eyes. Trees, flowers, children, husband, work, all looked different. I had new glasses, with no tint to distort what was there. For nearly two years I coasted in this newness of life, in a greater creativity than I had ever known, in work I loved. Then on waking one morning, I heard: "Come now, let us go." God was gently asking me to come to a deeper experience by returning to a more committed prayer life. My heart was "troubled" and I was "afraid" of getting off the path

again, afraid the prince of this world would dis-
tract me again. Yet I knew the Father would tell
me "exactly" what to do. Many years have passed
and the sense of the indwelling God remains.
There are temptations to leave the path; there are
daily struggles with being "in the world" rather
than "of the world"; but the words of Jesus have
never failed to lead me back to the Father.

Catherine's writing reveals one of the surprises of "di-rected" free-writing. While the passage from John inspired her to begin, the result was more than she expected. Her writing shows the broad strokes of personal, social and spiritual history. With this summary of her life, she could expand into numerous chapters about each stage of her life as presented in this single writing effort.

Reflections after Spiritual Reading

Some persons may feel uneasy using biblical texts if they have little experience with scripture. Prior to Vatican II, many lay people had little confidence in reading or studying scriptures. Yet, we were encouraged to read the works of the saints and spiritual writers. Thomas Merton re-popularized spiritual autobiography with the publica-tion of *The Seven Storey Mountain*. Often by way of jour-nal entries, Merton was led to record not only his growth as a monk, but thoughts that greatly influenced the world outside the Abbey of Gethsemani. By keeping a notebook we, too, can explore through writing what Merton calls the "different levels of depth." These levels will provide yet another approach to discovering the Mystery behind our stories.

First, there is the slightly troubled surface of the sea. Here there is action. I make plans. They toss in the wake of others' traffic: passing liners. I speak to the novices. I make resolutions to speak less wildly, to say fewer of the things that surprise myself and them. Where do they spring from?

Second, there is the darkness that comes when I close my eyes. Here is where the big, blue, purple, green, and gray fish swim by. Most beautiful and peaceful darkness: is it the cave of my own inner being? In this watercavern I easily live, whenever I wish. Dull rumors only of the world reach me. Sometimes a drowned barrel floats into the room. . . . It is comfortable. It is a rest. I half open my eyes to the sun, praising the Lord of glory. Lo, thus I have returned from the blank abyss, re-entering the shale cities of Genesis. . . . The question of socialization does not concern these waters. They are nobody's property. Animality. Game preserve. Paradise. No questions whatever perturb their holy botany. Neutral territory. No one's sea. I think God intended me to write about this second level, however, rather than the first. . . .

Third level. Here is the positive life swimming in the rich darkness which is no longer thick like water but pure, like air. Starlight, and you do not know where it is coming from. . . . Everything is charged with intelligence, though all is night. There is no speculation here. There is vigilance; life itself has turned to purity in its own refined depths. Everything is spirit. Here God is adored, God's coming is recognized, God is received as soon as God is expected and because God is expected God is received, but God has passed by sooner than God arrived. God was gone before God came. God returned forever. . . . In the wind of God's passing the angels cry "The Holy One is gone." Therefore I lie dead in the air of their wings. . . .

Here is where love burns with innocent flame, the clean desire for death: death without sweetness, without sickness, without commentary, without reference and without shame. . . . Know that there is in each of us a deep will, potentially committed to freedom or captivity, ready to consent to life, born consenting to death, turned inside out, swallowed by its own self, prisoner of itself like Jonas in the whale.[3]

After reading the excerpt by Merton, make a jotted (informal) outline of the surface events that are taking place in your life at the present moment. Then sit quietly, closing your eyes for ten or fifteen minutes. Pick up your notebook and describe what happened when you entered the second level, when you became still. What did you see in your "watercavern"? When have you experienced Merton's third level? Describe as fully as possible a moment, in the past or, perhaps, more recently in which you "received" God.

Life Review

Anthony De Mello began his book of meditations, *Wellsprings,* by asking the reader to make a review of his life.[4] I offer a slight adaptation of his meditation as an outline for approaching the entire story of one's life. Father De Mello has struck every chord possible in his wide range of suggestions for looking back over one's life. I present it for the sake of closure, yet this meditation is only the beginning of the search for God's timing in our individual and collective life stories.

Find a comfortable and quiet place where you can be alone for an hour or more. Have soothing music (without words) playing in the background. Slowly read Father De Mello's meditation, letting your mind dwell on each phrase for as long as you wish. After you have reflected for a few moments on each phrase of the whole meditation, jot down brief responses to each phrase. Later, when you have time to write again, pick one phrase at a time and explore it as fully as possible in a free-writing manner.

- *These things I have loved in Life:*
  Things I tasted:
  Things I looked at:
  Things I have smelled:
  Things I have heard:
  Things I have touched:

- *The following are experiences I have cherished in my childhood, in my school years, in early adulthood, in my present life:*
  These persons are enshrined within my heart:
  Ideas that have brought me liberation:
  Beliefs I have outgrown:
  Convictions I have lived by:
  Things I have lived for:

- *Insights I have gained in the school of life:*
  Insights into God:
  Insights into the world:
  Insights into human nature:

Insights into Love:
Insights into religion:

- *The following influences have shaped my life:*
  Persons:
  Occupations:
  Books:
  Events:

- *These are the risks I have taken, the dangers I have courted:*

- *These are the sufferings that have seasoned me:*

- *These are the lessons life has taught me:*

- *These words or scriptures have provided light for my journey:*

- *These are my life's achievements:*

- *Things I regret about my life:*

- *My unfulfilled desires:*

8

THE MYSTERY OF HEALING

If writing is thinking and discovery and selection and order and meaning, it is also awe and reverence and mystery and magic.[1]

These words of African-American novelist Toni Morrison compress into one sentence the essence of *The Mystery of My Story*. In a 1986 series of talks by six American writers, Morrison revealed the significant role of autobiography in crafting her novels. In exploring her personal history she was able to transcend her private world and enter the collective history of her people. Even for novice writers, the mystery beneath all our stories unfolds as we dare to write. The memory-jogging techniques explained in earlier chapters stimulate thinking and that thinking produces more writing. As we write and think, we begin to make a conscious selection of those stories we will flesh out in full detail. Once we have completed the exercises, we are ready to choose an order for presenting our life story. The order may be based on a framework, such as Erikson's or Levinson's psychosocial stages, or Merton's ''levels of depth,'' or the format of De Mello's life review. A person with an exceptionally varied work history may view her life from that perspective; another may have lived in many regions throughout the United States and other parts of the world and the thread of his story may be those different environments. Even though the process described in this work is thematic, the writer may choose, in the end, the more traditional and standard chronological approach. Whatever order we choose, the ordering of our material will create meaning. At the heart of meaning is the discovery of "awe and reverence and mystery and magic." The reader courageous enough to write the exercises suggested throughout this work will drink of the awe and reverence and mystery of their lives. The only magic lies in the ease with which our pens reveal that mystery.

Writing can become a rehearsal for expressing orally our stories to another. Fr. Gabriel Calvo, founder of the internationally presented Marriage Encounter experience, well understood writing as a tool for beginning or reopening dialogue among married couples as a source of enrichment and healing. After each presentation of content, couples are asked to write letters to one another addressing specific questions that relate to married life. After a private time of writing, the couple exchanges notebooks and reads the letters. Only then does the verbal dialogue begin. Privately expressing thoughts and memories on paper often releases the emotional content so that the telling comes more easily. Writing also gives the quiet person a chance to say all that needs saying as Susan, a social anthropologist, affirms:

> The act of writing my life events empowers me; I can do it on my own at any time; I don't need an appointment with some one. Inspiration comes through me, giving me self-confidence. As an introvert, it's easier to express myself in writing.

When we share life events with another, the listener is also reminded of her story. How often have we felt compelled to relate personal incidents to coworkers and acquaintances only to discover they have similar stories to share. At My Story workshops, a two-hour lunch break informally allows participants to share the memories they penned that morning. Key to sharing our stories is finding persons who are willing to listen without judgment. Support is a vital means of relating and healing life's traumas and illnesses.

In the earliest times, all the telling was oral. That's how the Israelites passed on their history. Stories traveled from one region to another in medieval days as warriors gathered in great halls to tell of brave knights and embattled kingdoms. Children never tire of hearing bedtime stories about their parents' early lives. The telling allows children to understand their past and connect that past to both present and future.

Writing as Healing

Perhaps the most profound effect of telling one's life story is the healing quality that comes first from discovering and secondly from giving expression to all the significant moments of our personal history. A diocesan director of spirituality, Rev. Patrick Eastman, explained the value of writing in both his professional work and his personal experience of the My Story workshop:

> *Individuals and communities are enriched and encouraged by getting in touch with the story of their own Salvation-history. We perceive this in the Hebrew Bible where the Jewish people are able, through the written word, to touch that which identifies them and calls them forth to new things. I find it helpful to encourage those who come for guidance to write their own story. It is helpful for me to begin to understand them, but it is even more useful for themselves. Some will be*

hesitant about writing, but this is important and has a different impact than a merely verbal account. The act of writing will often unearth many forgotten memories and the positive dimensions are very encouraging. Our past history informs the present and gives hope for the future. The process also uncovers negative material we have suppressed. Writing it down, however painful, puts it outside ourselves and is the beginning of the catharsis that detaches us from the destructive material held in our psyche, spirit and body. I discovered for myself the value of this encounter with my own salvation history in a My Story workshop. Being put in touch with myself through writing was a time of spiritual experience and growth.

Catharsis is a common effect of writing for personal and spiritual development. During a recent winter workshop, a young professional declared he wanted to leave after the first hour because the writing and remembering were too painful. As the weekend progressed, he made discoveries and connections which led to healing. He explained he had been in therapy for six months and hadn't made much progress. In the first hour of the workshop the root of his depression poured easily onto paper, a traumatic incident that happened at the age of five.

He expressed his gratitude and an eagerness to share his discovery with his therapist. He left the workshop at peace; he had solved the riddle of his depression. A month later he called to say his therapy was finished. The veil had lifted and he felt alive again.

At the closing celebration of one workshop, a recently widowed woman created the symbol of a gate to express her reality on that particular day. Through writing she realized she had spent her whole life pleasing parents, husband, children, and now grandchildren. While writing about her childhood, she discovered many interests she had never pursued because she put her life on hold to take care of everyone's needs but her own. She joked as she left the workshop, "My children may not like the new me. I don't want to babysit all the time; I want to go back to school, use some of the creativity I've always had but never used. I want to join others in sharing common interests. My children will have to begin handling their own lives. This is a birth day for me."

Kay, cofounder of a spiritual renewal center, reflected on the benefits of recording and sharing her life story:

> *Several months after the My Story workshop, I am aware of the healing dimension of some of the writings we did in the workshop as well as my recent efforts to record my story. Unlocking the door to that part of myself which feels free to talk about inner feelings, past memories, persons, places, happenings, without the overweening presence of my well-developed "critical, analytical overseer" who is almost always in the Chairman's seat in my life, is proving not only refreshing, it is life giving! The workshop's focus on the person's own life story is something I have long pushed away from consciously admitting. Even after meeting my husband and hearing all of his stories, I resisted expressing "my story."*
>
> *Accepting myself and others in the humanness lived out in what we talk about when we tell "our story" has come slowly but steadily. I am now much more ready and able to accept the reality of my story. During that time of sharing my husband's*

story, we both experienced a growing, healing, loving process toward a greater acceptance of life, a sense of being accepted as persons, and expanding borders of trust. Since the workshop, I have faced challenges tougher than any in the past thirteen years together. Our sense of trust in each other, along with the writing of my stories, enabled me to go through my stuff with a sense of human relatedness into which, from time to time, has been breathed a sense of spirit, a divine relatedness.

Kay's writing shows the benefits of using the prewriting techniques of listing, clustering or mind-mapping. These freed her from the inner critic. The "Chairman" was kept at a distance, allowing her to make associations and connections without editorial intrusion.

Writing your life story will take the rest of your life. Even after we have finished the telling up to this point in time, writing remains a powerful tool for continued growth and healing. One year after her My Story workshop, Elizabeth, a young mother expressed the value of continuing her notebook:

Dear God, What's bothering me? Christmas anxiety—and none of it is about You, the real Christmas. Yet, when I think of serving others, I feel I can barely take care of myself and family. How do you volunteer with two small children who have one ear infection after another? Even if I had the money do I pay so someone else can take care of my kids while I go be charitable? Make me submissive to my kids' schedule, make me patient and open.

*Guilt isn't from you, but I feel badly that I
can't feed the hungry, shelter the homeless. I have
a hard time just getting out to visit Grandma and
the old people who love to see my children. I need
to go back to the nursing home, don't I? It's okay
that Grandma doesn't know me—it hurts. Why
does she have to live this way? Why can't she just
join You? . . . My pen writes by itself and I am
always surprised at what comes out. I didn't know
that it bothered me that Grandma doesn't know me
because she always enjoys our company anyway.
Thanks, God, for revealing yourself (and myself)
to me.*

When Elizabeth is ready to order and thus create meaning out of the material in her notebooks, she will have in
this entry part of her grandmother's story; she will also see
the pattern of her struggle to find God in the inmost self
where healing begins and ends. In our seeking, it's difficult
to believe Paul's reminder to the Ephesians: "We are God's
work of art, created in Christ Jesus to live the good life as
from the beginning he has meant us to live it." [*Jerusalem Bible*]

Before returning this small volume to the bookshelf,
let's see in this final exercise what you have discovered as
you journeyed on paper through your life. In your notebook
or on a sheet of plain paper, print your full name in the
middle of the page. Circle your name and then cluster
around it all the words that come to mind. On this cluster
place your talents, desires, achievements, unfulfilled
dreams. Then take up a clean page; consider this page the
canvas on which you will paint a self-portrait. Using the
clustered words as a guide, describe the work of art God has
made of you. Are you circles or squares, triangles, spirals,

broad strokes or fine lines? What colors splash across the canvas of your life? As a closing My Story exercise an art teacher in her early forties wrote:

> *I have watched and marveled as the Geraldine of birth has changed into Gerry with a "y" to Gerri with an "i." The wonder of conversion through unexplainable pain, frosted with a light touch of joy here and there. I have seen pastels of color give way to the intensity and blooms of red, orange and yellow; toned again with awareness and understanding into subtle shades of mauves, purples, and the nothingness of white. I am at a transition of my life, major in its scope and meaningful in its thrust. The hiddenness of its outcome perplexing, and unsettling in its rumblings. I keep moving, one step ahead, perhaps two steps behind, with a knowingness of heart and a nothingness of mind. A journey of fear and fantasy: the unknown of mind versus the longing of the heart. The canvas has been gessoed, the new painting has begun. Dare I hope for a masterpiece?*

The portrait of our lives remains unfinished until we breathe for the last time. Our healing will not be complete until we have finished the paschal mystery of which we daily partake on the road back home, back into the Mystery from which our being springs. The journey through childhood, through years of school and work, the journey into old age: all can be set down as a matter of record. We may leave it to sisters and brothers, friends and relatives, perhaps to children and their children. With us into that gentle night will go the Holy Mystery that carries us through every word of our story.

NOTES

1. Unfinished Stories

1. Morton Kelsey, foreword to Paul Marechal, *Dancing Madly Backwards*. New York: Crossroad, 1982. xi.
2. Tristine Ranier. *The New Diary*. New York: Tarcher, 1978. 229.
3. John A. Sanford. *The Man Who Wrestled With God*. New York: Paulist, 1981. 1.
4. Herwig Arts. *With Your Whole Soul*. New York: Paulist, 1983. 28.
5. Sanford, 4.

2. Finding a Way

1. Dorothy Day. *The Long Loneliness*. New York: Harper, 1981. 10–11.
2. Samuel Pepys. "The Great Fire." *The Norton Anthology of English Literature*. Ed. M.H. Abrams. New York: Norton, 1986. 1852.
3. Pepys, 1852.
4. Thomas Merton. *The Sign of Jonas*. New York: Harcourt, 1981. 17.
5. Erik Erikson. *Childhood and Society*. New York: Norton, 1963. 254.
6. Erikson, 261.
7. Erikson, 264.
8. Erikson, 268.

9. Daniel Levinson. *The Seasons of a Man's Life*. New York: Ballantine, 1978. 18.
10. Levinson, 19.
11. John Dunne. *Search for God in Time and Memory*. Notre Dame: Notre Dame UP, 1977. 169–170.

3. Discovering the Persons We Used To Be

1. Eudora Welty. *One Writer's Beginnings*. Cambridge: Harvard UP, 1984. 103.
2. Joan Didion. *Slouching Towards Bethlehem*. New York: Washington Square, 1981. 142–143.
3. Thomas Merton. *The Seven Storey Mountain*. New York: Harcourt, 1948. 391.

4. Tapping the Wellsprings

1. Arts, 14.
2. C.G. Jung. *Memories, Dreams, Reflections*. New York: Random House, 1963. 6.
3. Jung, 7.
4. Jung, 8.
5. Arts, 13.
6. Arts, 15.
7. Arts, 22–23.
8. Arts, 29.
9. Didion, 142.
10. Arts, 30.
11. Day, 18.
12. Meinrad Craighead. *The Mother's Songs*. New York: Paulist, 1987. Intro.
13. Arts, 13.

14. Macrina Wiederkehr. *A Tree Full of Angels*. New York: Harper, 1988. 3–4.

5. Choosing Ourselves

1. Edward Connery Latham, ed. *The Poetry of Robert Frost*. New York: Holt, 1969.
2. Simone Weil. *Waiting for God*. New York: Harper, 1973. 51.
3. Carl Rogers. *On Becoming a Person*. New York: Houghton, 1961. 17.
4. Rogers, 16.
5. Rogers, 16.
6. Rogers, 17.
7. Rogers, 18.
8. Rogers, 20.
9. Rogers, 21.

6. When God Breaks Through

1. William James, quoted in Richard A. Nenneman, ''The Spiritual Element.'' *World Monitor*. April 1989: 79.
2. William Wordsworth. ''Ode on Intimations of Immortality.''
3. William Blake. *Songs of Innocence and of Experience*. New York: Oxford UP, 1988. Plate 30.
4. Jung, Introduction, x.
5. Jung, 20.
6. Benedict Groeschel. *Spiritual Passages*. New York: Crossroad, 1988. 68.
7. Kierkegaard, quoted in Groeschel, 132.
8. Day, 18.
9. Alister Hardy, quoted in, Nenneman, 79.

7. *Transforming and Transcending*

1. Albert E. Stone. *Autobiographical Occasions and Original Acts.* Philadelphia: U of Pennsylvania Press, 1982. 59.
2. Merton, *Sign of Jonas,* 338–39.
3. Merton, *Sign of Jonas,* 338–40.
4. Anthony De Mello. *Wellsprings.* New York: Doubleday, 1984. 14–15.

8. *The Mystery of Healing*

1. Quoted in William Zinsser, ed. *Inventing the Truth: The Art and Craft of Memoir.* Boston: Houghton, 1987. 111.

REFERENCES

Arts, Herwig, S.J. *With Your Whole Soul.* New York: Paulist, 1983.

Blake, William. *Songs of Innocence and of Experience.* New York: Oxford University Press, 1988.

Craighead, Meinrad. *The Mother's Songs.* New York: Paulist, 1987.

Daggy, Robert E., ed. *Introduction East and West: The Foreign Prefaces of Thomas Merton.* Greensboro: Unicorn Press, 1981.

Day, Dorothy. *The Long Loneliness.* New York: Harper, 1981.

De Mello, Anthony. *Wellsprings.* New York: Doubleday, 1986.

Dunne, John. *Search for God in Time and Memory.* Notre Dame: Notre Dame UP, 1977.

Erikson, Erik. *Childhood and Society.* New York: Norton, 1963.

Groeschel, Benedict. *Spiritual Passages.* New York: Crossroad, 1988.

Jung, C.G. *Memories, Dreams, Reflections.* New York: Random House, 1963.

Kelsey, Morton. Foreword. *Dancing Madly Backwards.* By Paul Marechal. New York: Crossroad, 1982.

Latham, Edward Connery, ed. *The Poetry of Robert Frost.* New York: Holt, 1969.

Levinson, Daniel. *The Seasons of a Man's Life.* New York: Ballantine, 1978.

Merton, Thomas. *The Seven Storey Mountain*. New York: Harcourt, 1948.

———. *The Sign of Jonas*. New York: Harcourt, 1981.

Nenneman, Richard A. "The Spiritual Element." *World Monitor*. April, 1989.

Ranier, Tristine. *The New Diary*. New York: Tarcher, 1978.

Rico, Gabriele Lusser. *Writing the Natural Way*. New York: Tarcher, 1983.

Rogers, Carl. *On Becoming a Person*. New York: Houghton, 1961.

Sanford, John A. *The Man Who Wrestled With God*. New York: Paulist, 1981.

Stone, Albert E. *Autobiographical Occasions and Original Acts*. Philadelphia: U of Pennsylvania Press, 1982.

Weil, Simone. *Waiting for God*. New York: Harper, 1973.

Welty, Eudora. *One Writer's Beginnings*. Cambridge: Harvard UP, 1984.

Zinsser, William, ed. *Inventing the Truth*. Boston: Houghton, 1987.